yajuok & Violet, Rome

Guc...
By D...

Spring 2024
Counter Histories

Words & Pictures

Front

Back

Front cover:
Studio photograph,
2000–2010, from Billy
H.C. Kwok's project *For
So Many Years When I
Close My Eyes*, 2022–23
Courtesy the artist
(See page 34)

Opposite:
Detail of surveillance
photograph, 1970, from
Christopher Gregory-
Rivera's series *Las
Carpetas*, 2014–ongoing
Courtesy the Archivo
General de Puerto Rico,
San Juan
(See page 58)

Subscribe to *Aperture* and
visit archive.aperture.org
for every issue since 1952.

Aperture is a nonprofit publisher dedicated to creating insight, community, and understanding through photography. Established in 1952 to advance "creative thinking, significantly expressed in words and photographs," Aperture champions photography's vital role in nurturing curiosity and encouraging a more just, tolerant society.

Aperture (ISSN 0003-6420) is published quarterly, in spring, summer, fall, and winter, at 548 West 28th Street, 4th Floor, New York, NY 10001. In the United States, a one-year subscription (four issues) is $75; a two-year subscription (eight issues) is $124. In Canada, a one-year subscription is $95. All other international subscriptions are $110 per year. Visit aperture.org to subscribe. Single copies may be purchased at $24.95 for most issues. Subscribe to the *Aperture Digital Archive* at aperture.org/archive. Periodicals postage paid at New York and additional offices. Postmaster: Send address changes to *Aperture*, PO Box 3000, Denville, NJ 07834. Address queries regarding subscriptions, renewals, or gifts to: *Aperture* Subscription Service, 866-457-4603 (US and Canada), or email custsvc_aperture@fulcoinc.com.

Newsstand distribution in the US is handled by CMG. For international distribution, contact Central Books, centralbooks.com. Other inquiries, email orders@aperture.org or call 212-505-5555.

Become a Member of Aperture to take your interest in and knowledge of photography further. With an annual tax-deductible gift of $250, membership includes a complimentary subscription to *Aperture* magazine, discounts on Aperture's award-winning publications, a special limited-edition gift, and more. To join, visit aperture.org/join, or contact membership@aperture.org.

Credits for "Curriculum," pp. 20–21: Canet cover: courtesy Jack Pierson; Scorsese and Tedeschi: courtesy Showtime; Schneider: © the artist

Printed in Turkey by Ofset Yapimevi

OFSET
YAPIMEVİ

Support has been provided by members of Aperture's Magazine Council: Jon Stryker and Slobodan Randjelović, Susan and Thomas Dunn, Kate Cordsen and Denis O'Leary, and Michael W. Sonnenfeldt, MUUS Collection.

The Counter Histories issue of *Aperture* magazine is supported, in part, by Magnum Foundation.

Magnum Foundation

aperture
The Magazine of Photography and Ideas

Statement of Ownership, Management, and Circulation (Required by 39 U.S.C. 3685). 1. Publication Title: Aperture; 2. Publication no.: 0003-6420; 3. Filing Date: October 5, 2023 4. Issue Frequency: Quarterly; 5. No. of Issues Published Annually: 4; 6. Annual Subscription Price: 75; 7. Complete Mailing Address of Known Office of Publication: Aperture, 548 West 28th Street, 4th Floor, New York, NY 10001-5511; Contact Person: Dana Triwush; Telephone: 212-946-7116; 8. Complete Mailing Address of Headquarters or General Business Office of Publisher: Aperture, 548 West 28th Street, 4th Floor, New York, NY 10001-5511; 9. Full Names and Complete Mailing Addresses of Publisher, Editor, and Managing Editor: Publisher: Dana Triwush, Aperture, 548 West 28th Street, 4th Floor, New York, NY 10001-5511; Editor: Michael Famighetti, Aperture, 548 West 28th Street, 4th Floor, New York, NY 10001-5511; Managing Editor: Varun Nayar, Aperture, 548 West 28th Street, 4th Floor, New York, NY 10001-5511; 10. Owner: Aperture Foundation, Inc., 548 West 28th Street, 4th Fl., New York, NY 10001; 11. Known Bondholders, Mortgagees, and Other Security Holders Owning or Holding 1 Percent or More of Total Amount of Bonds, Mortgages, or Other Securities: None; 12. Tax Status: The purpose, function, and nonprofit status of this organization and the exempt status for federal income tax purposes: Has Not Changed During Preceding 12 Months; 13. Publication Title: Aperture; 14. Issue Date for Circulation Data Below: 06/06/2023; 15. Extent and Nature of Circulation (Average No. Copies Each Issue During Preceding 12 Months; No. Copies of Single Issue Published Nearest to Filing Date): a. Total Number of Copies (Net press run): 13,749; 15,053; b. Paid Circulation; (1) Mailed Outside-County Paid Subscriptions Stated on PS Form 3541: 5,707; 5,786; (2) Mailed In-County Paid Subscriptions Stated on PS Form 3541: 0; 0; (3) Paid Distribution Outside the Mails Including Sales Through Dealers and Carriers, Street Vendors, Counter Sales, and Other Paid Distribution Outside USPS: 3,375; 3,206; (4) Paid Distribution by Other Classes of Mail Through the USPS: 10; 10; c. Total Paid Distribution: 9,092; 9,002; d. Free or Nominal Rate Distribution: (1) Free or Nominal Rate Outside-County Copies included on PS Form 3541: 381; 406; (2) Free or Nominal Rate In-County Copies Included on PS From 3541: 0; 0; (3) Free or Nominal Rate Copies Mailed at Other Classes Through the USPS: 82; 81; (4) Free or Nominal Rate Distribution Outside the Mail: 188; 72; e. Total Free or Nominal Rate Distribution: 651; 559; f. Total Distribution: 9,743; 9,561; g. Copies not Distributed: 4,005; 5,492; h. Total: 13,748; 15,053; i. Percent Paid 93.32%; 94.15%; 16. Electronic Copy Circulation, a. Paid Electronic Copies: 1,011; 1,142; b. Total Paid Print Copies + Paid Electronic Copies: 10,103; 10,144; c. Total Print Distribution + Paid Electronic Copies: 10,754; 10,703; d. Percent Paid (Both Print & Electronic Copies): 93.94%; 94.78%; I certify that 50% of all my distributed copies (Electronic & Print) are paid above a nominal price. 17. Publication of Statement of Ownership: Will be printed in the 03/05/2024 issue of this publication. 18. I certify that all information furnished on this form is true and complete. I understand that anyone who furnishes false or misleading information on this form or who omits material or information requested on the form may be subject to criminal sanctions (including fines and imprisonment) and/or civil sanctions (including civil penalties). Signature and Title of Editor, Publisher, Business Manager, or Owner: Dana Triwush, Publisher, October 5, 2023

aperture.org

THE PHⓄTO GRAPHY SHOW

PRESENTED BY AIPAD

RETURNS TO
THE PARK AVENUE ARMORY
APRIL 25 – 28, 2024

643 PARK AVE
NEW YORK CITY

aipad

The Association of International
Photography Art Dealers

WWW.AIPAD.COM
INFO@AIPAD.COM
@AIPADPHOTO

EXHIBITING GALLERIES 2024
°CLAIRbyKahn, Zurich
19th Century Rare Book & Photograph Shop, New York
Arnika Dawkins Gallery, Atlanta
Assembly, Houston
Augusta Edwards Fine Art, London
Baudoin Lebon, Paris
BILDHALLE, Zurich | Amsterdam
Bruce Silverstein Gallery, New York
Candela Gallery, Richmond
Catherine Couturier Gallery, Houston
Cavalier Gallery, New York
Charles Isaacs Photographs Inc, New York
CLAMP, New York
Contemporary Works/Vintage Works, Chalfont
Daniel / Oliver Gallery, Brooklyn
Danziger Gallery, New York | Los Angeles
Deborah Bell Photographs, New York
Duncan Miller Gallery, Los Angeles
Edwynn Houk Gallery, New York
ELLEPHANT, Montreal
Etherton Gallery, Tucson
Fisheye Gallery, Paris | Arles
Foto Relevance, Houston
Galería RocioSantaCruz, Barcelona
Galerie Catherine et André Hug, Paris
Galerie Clémentine de la Feronnière, Paris
Galerie Esther Woerdehoff, Paris
Galerie Johannes Faber, Vienna
Galerie Olivier Waltman, Paris
Galerie SIT DOWN, Paris
Galerie XII, Santa Monica | Paris
Gallery 270, Westwood
Gitterman Gallery, New York
Grob Gallery, Geneva
G.W. Einstein Company, New York
HackelBury Fine Art Limited, London
Hans P. Kraus Jr. Inc., New York
Higher Pictures, Brooklyn
Holden Luntz Gallery, Palm Beach
Howard Greenberg Gallery, New York
The Hulett Collection, Tulsa
IBASHO, Antwerp
Ilaria Quadrani Fine Arts, New York
Ippodo Gallery, New York
Jackson Fine Art, Atlanta
jdc Fine Art, San Diego
Joseph Bellows Gallery, La Jolla
Keith de Lellis Gallery, New York
La Galerie de l'Instant, Paris
Laurence Miller Gallery, New York
Les Douches la Galerie, Paris
Magnum Photos Gallery, Paris
Marshall Gallery, Santa Monica
Michael Hoppen Gallery, London
Michael Shapiro Photographs, Westport
MIYAKO YOSHINAGA, New York
MOMENTUM, Miami
Monroe Gallery of Photography, Santa Fe
Nailya Alexander Gallery, New York
Obscura Gallery, Santa Fe
PACI contemporary, Brescia
Paul M. Hertzmann, Inc., San Francisco
Peter Fetterman Gallery, Santa Monica
Photo Discovery, Paris
Robert Klein Gallery, Boston
Robert Koch Gallery, San Francisco
Robert Mann Gallery, New York
Scheinbaum & Russek Ltd, Santa Fe
Scott Nichols Gallery, Sonoma
Staley-Wise Gallery, New York
Stephen Bulger Gallery, Toronto
Stephen Daiter Gallery, Chicago
The Third Gallery Aya, Osaka
Throckmorton Fine Art, New York
Todd Webb Archive, Portland
Toluca Fine Art, Paris
Vasari, Buenos Aires
Von Lintel Gallery, Santa Monica
Yancey Richardson, New York

Robert Polidori | Courtesy of Edwynn Houk Gallery

M|C|A PHOTOGRAPHY

mica.edu/aperture

**Phylicia Ghee '10
(Photography & Curatorial
Studies BFA)**

phyliciaghee.com

"My work is a representation of
my lineage. My grandfather's
fingerprint has left an indelible
mark on my practice—much like
the ink of my mother's pen, the
stitches of my grandmother's
needle, the patchwork legacy
of my great-grandmother's
quilting, and the whispers of
my great-great-grandmother's
herbal remedies. These
elements trail down my lineage,
ultimately finding me in dreams
interlaced with memories
that influence my artistic and
photographic inclinations."

Khepri: I am because You are #2,
A series honoring my Grandfather, Ghee

Agenda
Exhibitions to See

Takuma Nakahira

A leading photographer and critic, Takuma Nakahira had a lasting impact on Japanese art after World War II, from his poetic images to his perceptive writing on art and his work as a founder of *Provoke*—an influential, short-lived magazine of experimental photographic expression. *Burn—Overflow*, a long-awaited exhibition organized by the National Museum of Modern Art, Tokyo, examines Nakahira's wide-ranging career through the perspective of his critical commitments and fascination with the tension between words and images. The show features more than four hundred works and documents, moving chronologically through five sections, from the *Provoke* era and Nakahira's first photobook, *For a Language to Come* (1970), to his engagements with urban space and landscape as an apparatus of political power, providing an expansive context for the photographer's radical social critique and haunting imagery.

Takuma Nakahira: Burn—Overflow at the National Museum of Modern Art, Tokyo, February 6–April 7, 2024

Takuma Nakahira, *The Streets, or Traces of Terror*, 1976
© Gen Nakahira

David Seidner

At age seventeen, David Seidner moved from Los Angeles to Paris to become a fashion photographer. He landed his first magazine cover two years later. Precocious and prolific, Seidner worked with the leading brands and magazines of the 1980s and '90s—Yves Saint Laurent, Revlon, *Vanity Fair*—and made strikingly moody portraits of artists including Robert Rauschenberg and Louise Bourgeois. "He was a true maker, deeply invested in process, printing, and the photograph as object," says Elisabeth Sherman, the director of exhibitions at the International Center of Photography, New York, which presents the first comprehensive exhibition of Seidner's work since his death, from AIDS-related illnesses, in 1999. At a time when fashion was cordoned off from fine art, Seidner collapsed genre boundaries, pursuing techniques of distortion, mirroring, and multiple exposures. "Seidner's ability to reinvent and experiment throughout his career," Sherman adds, "resonates with today's contemporary landscape where evolution is an increasing pressure for artists."

David Seidner, *Francine Howell, Azzedine Alaïa*, 1986
© David Seidner Archive and the International Center of Photography, New York

David Seidner: Fragments, 1977–99 at the International Center of Photography, New York, January 26–May 6, 2024

David Goldblatt

Several years ago, David Goldblatt was making a photograph by the side of the road between Johannesburg and Cape Town when a car stopped and a man got out. The man's wife had recognized Goldblatt from television. "You make us see what we don't notice," the man said. Throughout his prolific career, Goldblatt described the intricate relationship between apartheid and the landscape in South Africa, where he photographed monumental structures built by white settlers, Black people dispossessed of their homes, night-shift workers on crowded trains, and ominous towers surveilling townships—always seeing the everyday details that revealed the profound impact of the country's political history. *David Goldblatt: No Ulterior Motive* takes a thematic approach, juxtaposing works made decades apart. The apartheid system tried to flatten nonwhite communities, the curator Judy Ditner notes, but Goldblatt's achievement was to "bear quiet witness to their individuality."

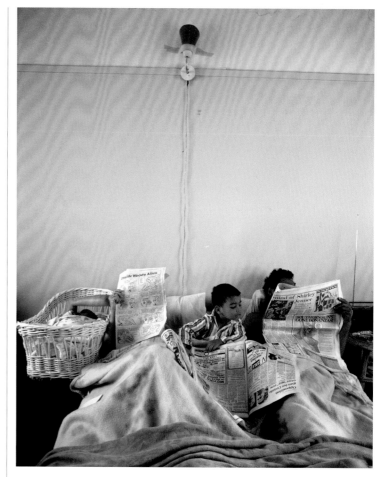

David Goldblatt: No Ulterior Motive **at Fundación MAPFRE, Madrid, May 29–September 1, 2024**

David Goldblatt, *Sunday morning: A not-white family living illegally in the "White" group area of Hillbrow, Johannesburg*, 1978
© the David Goldblatt Legacy Trust

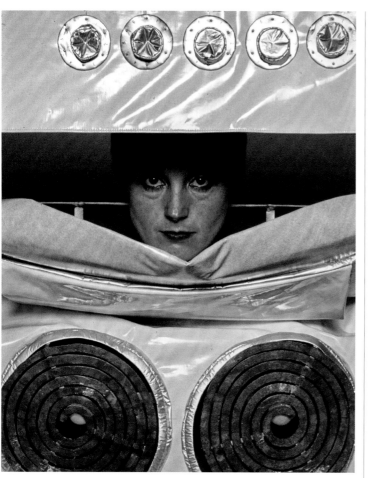

Helen Chadwick, *In the Kitchen (Stove)*, 1977
© Helen Chadwick Estate and courtesy Richard Saltoun Gallery, London

Women in Revolt!

The writer Lola Olufemi once declared that "feminist activists have always pushed boundaries set by the state, by men, by the powerful, and in doing so, laid the foundations for a new world." Showcasing the pivotal role of feminist art in shaping British culture, *Women in Revolt!* at Tate Britain covers the groundbreaking contributions of women artists in the UK between 1970 and 1990. The show presents works by more than one hundred artists in media ranging from photography, painting, drawing, sculpture, and film, and traces their contributions to major social and political movements from the beginning of the women's liberation movement through early struggles for civil rights, the AIDS crisis, and finally the Thatcher era. Artist by artist, this sweeping exhibition gives due credit to women whose work has undergirded decades of social progress.

Women in Revolt! Art and Activism in the UK 1970–1990 **at Tate Britain, London, November 8, 2023–April 7, 2024**

Make Prints

Skink Ink Fine Art Printing

Edition & Exhibition Printmakers
For Artists & Photographers

Tel: 646 455 3400 | Email: Services@skink.ink | Web: Skink.ink

Frank Stewart (b. 1949); *The Bow, Modena, Italy* [DETAIL], 1996; inkjet print; collection of Andre Kimo Stone Guess and Cheryl Peterson Guess.

INVESTMENT PROVIDED BY:

Frank Stewart's NEXUS

AN AMERICAN PHOTOGRAPHER'S JOURNEY, 1960s TO THE PRESENT

FEBRUARY 9–MAY 12 | SAVANNAH, GA | TELFAIR.ORG

The exhibition is co-organized by The Phillips Collection and Telfair Museums and curated by Ruth Fine and Fred Moten. This exhibition is supported in part by the National Endowment for the Arts.

JEPSON CENTER
TELFAIR MUSEUMS

Viewfinder

Three decades ago, Mariko Mori spoofed gender roles in Japan through playful performances staged in locations around Tokyo.

Marigold Warner

It is 1994 in Tokyo and Mariko Mori is angry. She has just come out of a business meeting, and is appalled to find that intelligent women, with degrees from leading universities, are being made to serve tea while working at the office. She has recently returned from five years overseas, studying art in London at the Chelsea College of Art and Design, followed by two years in New York at the Whitney Museum's rigorous Independent Study Program. "I was exposed to seeing the position of women in the West," she recalled in a recent conversation with me, speaking from her home in New York. "I was shocked. I wanted to demonstrate, as a social criticism, the lack of equality for women in Japan."

Dressed in a silver bodysuit with pointy ears, Mori sets out to Shinjuku, Tokyo's busiest business district. She clacks along the sidewalk in her patent heels and pinafore, carrying a tray of green tea in porcelain cups and saucers. She smiles and serves dutifully, as businessmen rush by on their morning commutes. The scene is at once comical and unsettling. Guised as a cyborg in a setting that epitomizes economic prosperity and power, Mori critiques the antiquated gender roles of corporate Japan and illustrates how women are alienated and othered in these spaces.

The performance culminated in a trilogy of still photographs, *Tea Ceremony I*, *II*, and *III* (1994). They are part of a wider body of work in which Mori adopts futuristic personas inspired by Japanese anime and pop culture. These images propelled Mori into the international spotlight. In 1995, at age twenty-eight, she held her first solo show at American Fine Arts, Co., New York, and two years later exhibited at the 47th Venice Biennale. Today, Mori's multidisciplinary art, characterized by a fascination with futurism, technology, and spirituality, is exhibited and collected by museums worldwide. Although now recognized as one of Japan's leading contemporary artists, she describes being ignored around the time the *Tea Ceremony* images were made. Not only was she disregarded by passersby during the performance, the series remained unexhibited in Japan until 2002, when it was shown at the Museum of Contemporary Art Tokyo. "Japanese society is collective," Mori explains. "We don't have such a strong culture of criticism. I don't think this work ever received a reaction from Japanese society. The reaction was mostly from the West."

Feminism has existed in Japan since the Meiji Restoration in the nineteenth century. However, its progression has been comparatively slow. In the United States, women's suffrage was achieved in 1920; in Japan, women did not gain the

Previous page:
Tea Ceremony I, 1994

This page:
Tea Ceremony II, 1994
© the artist and courtesy
Sean Kelly, New York

Mori's costume, inspired by her favorite childhood anime character, reveals an interrogation of gendered dress codes.

right to vote until 1947. A similar pattern can be seen in the art world. Women artists in the postwar era, such as Atsuko Tanaka of the Gutai group, Yuki Katsura, and Yoshiko Shimada, actively responded to feminist thought, but it was not until the 1990s that their work was recognized, when Japanese critics and curators began to consider art from a feminist perspective.

In that context, Mori's *Tea Ceremony* was radical in its overt criticism of gender inequality. This critique is, sadly, still relevant: in government, women make up just 8 percent of the ruling party. "It really was worse," Mori reflects on the moment she made this work. "But the fundamental structure is still there today. We need to deconstruct that concept that has been inherited through history; otherwise, it's not going to change."

Over the last few decades, working women in Japan have experienced, paradoxically, liberation and oppression. The pay gap has shrunk by a third, and while policies to diversify leadership positions have been put in place, women continue to face discriminatory hiring practices. A closer look at Mori's costume, inspired by her favorite childhood anime character, Astro Boy, reveals an interrogation of persistent gendered dress codes. Her button-up pinafore and high heels signal the cultural icon of the "office lady": a female employee of corporate

Japan, colloquially abbreviated to OL (*o-eru*). Japanese companies are notorious for standards of dress that have been reported to include guidelines on the height of heels and a requirement to wear makeup. Back in the 1990s, women were treated as low-skilled clerical workers, despite their being equally educated in comparison to their male counterparts. They were paid substantially less, and their jobs consisted mainly of answering phones, entering data, and making tea. Today, there are more opportunities for women, but the behavioral expectations illustrated by Mori—of modesty, tidiness, courtesy, and compliance—remain firmly embedded in the national psyche.

In Japan, feminism has not flooded the collective consciousness in the same way it has in the West. Perhaps artists offer some hope. Feminist photographers such as Yurie Nagashima, Ishiuchi Miyako, and Tomoko Sawada are receiving renewed recognition for their work, and a younger generation of artists, such as the collective Tomorrow Girls Troop, is speaking out. "Artists have the ability to project a future vision," says Mori. "We have a responsibility to imagine a better future, because if we can't imagine it, we will never make it."

Marigold Warner is a writer based in Tokyo.

Dispatches

Will accelerating economic disparity threaten Vancouver as a vital creative hub?
Aaron Peck

For much of last summer, the mountains on the North Shore appeared to buffer Vancouver from the smoke of forest fires that had engulfed the rest of Canada. Even with its summer breeze of cedar and sea, the city felt uneasy. In particular, the infamously down-and-out Downtown Eastside—with its single-room occupancy rentals, its dive bars, its fentanyl, crack, and heroin, its encampments that police periodically remove, its alleys of the unhoused—had never seemed more on edge. Vancouverites accept a certain level of grit and abjection, which comes through in images by the city's most celebrated photographers, from Fred Herzog to Greg Girard, but the atmosphere feels different after the pandemic. Even my wife, who grew up in Strathcona, the residential neighborhood adjacent to the Downtown Eastside, told me on our return visit last summer that for the first time in her life she didn't feel safe in the area. I removed my headphones when walking down Hastings Street.

On the edge of Strathcona rests Jeff Wall's studio, where I spent an afternoon with the artist. We discussed his new works, particularly three pieces being prepared for his 2024 retrospective at the Beyeler Foundation, near Basel. Wall's recent tableaux impress me in how they continue to push what a photograph is capable of picturing, the bodies of his subjects often caught in microgestures difficult for the eye to see, or depicting things otherwise impossible. (I would still love for him to return to self-portraiture, though.) We also looked at another unfinished piece, in digital form, a sort of development of an earlier series that pictures scenes from literary sources.

After our time in the studio, we walked into Strathcona. Sitting on a café patio, we watched the photographer Jennilee Marigomen cross Keefer Street with her son. Around that time, Marigomen, a frequent contributor to the *New York Times*, had been posting stories on her Instagram account about the Online News Act, a 2023 Canadian law that requires tech companies to compensate news outlets with revenue from shared links. In July 2023, in response to the legislation, which had passed into law the previous month, Google and Meta began blocking Canadian media content from their platforms, making it more difficult for young talent to establish themselves as practitioners through local news outlets, as their reportage will no longer circulate on social media. It is yet one more concern for artists calibrating the tedious hustle of a globalized city, where the cost of one-bedroom rentals has increased by 16 percent in the past year alone. Luxury condos sprout throughout the downtown core, as overdose centers close. "The shape of a city," wrote Charles Baudelaire, "changes, alas, more quickly than the human heart."

Many social, economic, and environmental problems facing artists in Vancouver may not feel new, but their intensity has increased. Ian Wallace's *Poverty* (1980–87) explored depictions of wealth inequality (ironically, the series was taken in Yaletown, which has since become one of the city's toniest neighborhoods). Evan Lee's *Forest Fires* (2009–10), made from photographs found online on which the artist manipulated printer's ink so that they resemble expressionist paintings, considers the aesthetics of landscape and destruction. Dana Claxton, who in 2020 won the Scotiabank Photography Award, often engages representations

Opposite:
Jeff Wall, *In the Legion,*
2022
Courtesy the artist

This page:
Stan Douglas, *Vancouver,*
***15 June 2011,* 2021**
© the artist and courtesy
Victoria Miro and David
Zwirner, New York

The city retains a strong photographic tradition, particularly from conceptual art and social critique, even reportage.

of Indigenous identity in popular culture. And most recently, at the 2022 Venice Biennale, Stan Douglas presented *Vancouver, 15 June 2011* (2021), a cinematically staged photograph of the 2011 Stanley Cup riots echoing Roy Arden's earlier video *Supernatural* (2005), made from footage of similar hockey riots in 1994.

To be sure, Vancouver retains a strong photographic tradition, particularly from conceptual art and social critique, even reportage, and has enough institutional support to foster it. The Polygon Gallery hosts the annual Philip B. Lind Emerging Artist Prize for British Columbia–based artists whose medium is photography, film, or video. In summer 2023, both the Polygon and the Vancouver Art Gallery announced new hires: Monika Szewczyk, known for her work with Allan Sekula, was appointed chief curator at the Polygon, and Eva Respini, previously at the Institute of Contemporary Art, Boston, and the photography department at the Museum of Modern Art, New York, became deputy director and director of curatorial programs at the Vancouver Art Gallery. I recently met with a former student from my years teaching at Emily Carr University of Art + Design who is now a practicing artist-photographer living in Brussels. We discussed how the pressure of rising costs and the city's relative remoteness make it a difficult place for young artists to build a practice, though I remain hopeful that Vancouver's cultural life will persevere through current uncertainties.

Late last August, weather patterns shifted. Smoke from wildfires in the Okanagan—the forested valley in which I grew up and that Marigomen photographed so beautifully for the *New York Times* in 2022—rolled over the peaks of the North Shore and reached the city. One afternoon, I watched a band of smog from the sky slowly lower until the mountains were no longer visible.

Aaron Peck's writing has appeared in the *Times Literary Supplement,* **The Believer, and** *Frieze.* **Originally from Vancouver, he now lives in Paris.**

Backstory

**Ketaki Sheth rediscovers her photographs of the bustling
center of 1990s-era Hindi cinema.**

Iva Dixit

In Bombay, the restless metropolis that houses India's twelve-billion-dollar Hindi cinema industry, the 1990s were a moment of roiling change. The cultural and visual excesses that had dictated the medium for the last decade were winding down, but the sheen of power and glamour remained. It was in this milieu that the young Bombay-based photographer Ketaki Sheth struck up a friendship with the prominent film critic Khalid Mohamed and found herself in the midst of the vast industry that is now somewhat coarsely referred to as "Bollywood."

From premiere parties where aspiring starlets jostled for attention to union rooms in which unemployed stuntmen played endless games of carrom, this was a world with its own language, hierarchies, and rules, and Sheth set about photographing it from the perspective of a curious outsider. This work remained mostly unseen by the public; Sheth herself rediscovered it purely by chance, while going through her archive. Today, when every aspect of a star's life is available for consumption via contractually negotiated paparazzi shots or Instagram reels of awkward dance challenges, there's a quiet dignity to these images, which let us see their subjects at their most human.

In Sheth's photograph of a twenty-seven-year-old Meenakshi Seshadri, each false eyelash on the classical-dancer-turned-actress's face exaggerates her petulant-ingenue half snarl toward the camera as she's caught unawares. Sheth told me she had been showing the photographer Lee Friedlander around Bombay's Film City, a sprawling studio complex where several films are often shot at once, when she spotted Seshadri leaving her set. In the resulting image, the actress is hedged in on one side by a tower of egg crates and flanked by two "spot boys," a Hindi film term for the men who act as chaperone-assistant-valet-nannies to lead actors (each has their own). A behemoth of an umbrella is brandished over Seshadri—one of a spot boy's main duties is to follow his charge around between takes, holding off the weather.

Sheth's camera finds the actor Shatrughan Sinha reclining in a chair, clad in the khadi kurta and dhoti of a villager. Sinha's slicked-back hair gleams, and his lowered eyes are hooded with a quiet menace, the same quality that earned him the nicknames "Shotgun" and "Shatru" ("enemy") in his heyday, when he was known for his flamboyant depictions of villainy.

One striking image is of Rekha, an immediately recognizable name to fans of Hindi cinema, regardless of generation. Over her life and career, the actress born Bhanurekha Ganesan achieved a level of fame accorded to very few women in popular culture. Now sixty-nine, she is only ever photographed in heavy heirloom Kanjeevaram sarees, her hair severely pulled back to reveal machete-like cheekbones seemingly impervious to age or gravity, a streak of red sindoor at the center of her militaristically straight part. Sheth's gloriously deceptive portrait, taken on a set in Juhu, Bombay, in 1988, ostensibly depicts a Rekha stripped of all such armor.

But, as Sheth recounted to me, Rekha "was fully focused on me and the shot and kept giving me angles that suited her and her cheekbones." Sheth listened to Rekha's directions but opted not to do a close-up of her iconic face,

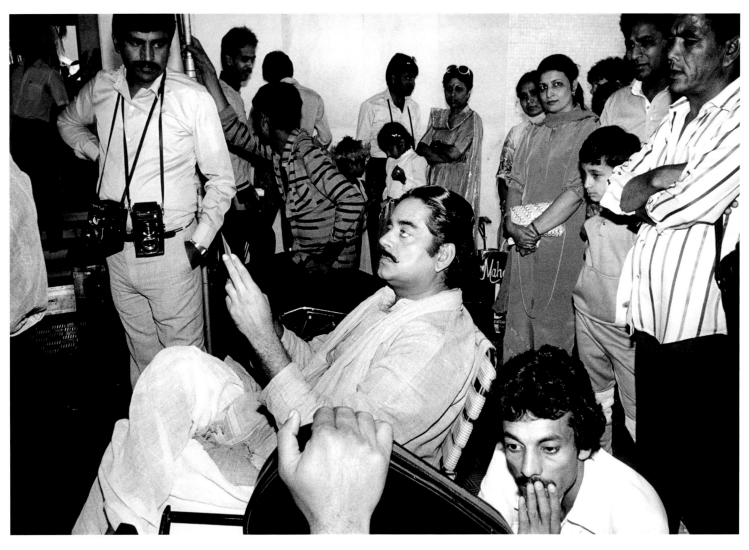

The actor Shatrughan Sinha
rehearsing lines, 1990
Courtesy the artist and
PHOTOINK, New Delhi

Sheth immortalizes ordinary moments from an extraordinary world.

instead deploying her lens to include the backdrop of a painting of clouds behind the actress and an empty birdcage in the foreground. "I wanted a moment which captured both her beauty and her solitude," Sheth says. Here, one of cinema's greatest sphinxlike stars appears almost lost, submerged in a painfully human daze of restlessness and boredom as she lounges casually in a plain white salwar kameez on a plush leather chair, her wrist resting on her forehead and her feet tucked below her in an affectation of uncommon vulnerability.

Whether documenting India's vanishing photography studios or the lives of the Sidi people (Indians of African origin), Sheth's work explores the intricacies of everyday labor—its loneliness, the spaces in which it is done, the rituals surrounding its performance. These photographs share the same inquiry, even if this time the laborers happen to be certain otherworldly beings. Conjuring Hindi cinema's specific form of dramatic grandeur onscreen and at the box office, Friday after Friday, is a loud, noisy, and frenetic business, one that takes an arsenal of extras, backup dancers, and stuntmen to execute. Sheth immortalizes

ordinary moments from an extraordinary world, capturing the celestial bodies at the center of this chaotic galaxy in rare moments of solitude on film sets, reveling in their hard-won pockets of silence even as the machinery of movie making thunders around them. Her portraits imbue these stars with the dignity of ordinariness. Here, they are mundane workers battling the demands of a surreal industry. Here, their bodies exhibit the fatigue their onscreen characters can never feel. Here, their faces display the weariness their celebrity does not permit them.

Iva Dixit is an editor and writer at the *New York Times Magazine*.

Curriculum
Jack Pierson

Oscar Wilde once wrote that every portrait is a portrait of the artist. That's certainly true for Jack Pierson, who has made numerous "self-portraits" that are, in fact, pictures of other people—mostly young men, lithe and well lit, replying to the camera with an interrogative gaze. Pierson came of age in Boston in the 1980s and became associated with the so-called Boston School alongside Nan Goldin, David Armstrong, and Philip-Lorca diCorcia. His career-long fascination with queer glamour has yielded a deep archive of singular portraiture, selections from which were on display in a recent exhibition in New York that also included drawings, posters, sculptures, and letters from vintage signs, one reading "REAL LIFE."

Bobbi Boyle and the Trio

Given that I have an inordinate fondness for the "also ran," the "other Supremes," and people who "were there" but had to inhabit their own glory, just to the side of superstardom, perhaps out of some ungrateful identification, I often find myself thinking, Why not Bobbi Boyle? Few things are as joy inducing to me as listening to *A Day in the Life*, this impeccable 1967 album of covers by a masterful Encino lounge singer and her trio. You can hear songs from this private-press record on YouTube— you won't find them on any of the principal streaming services.

The Razor's Edge

The Razor's Edge, directed by Edmund Goulding and released in 1946, is a movie I repeatedly return to for solace and respite from contemporary life. Based on W. Somerset Maugham's 1944 novel of the same name, it tracks the odyssey of a World War I fighter pilot, Larry Darrell, after he returns to the United States, determined not to adjust to the status quo. He makes a beeline out of high society and into, as Elliott Templeton, his fiancée's uncle and a favorite character of mine, snarls, "the hoi polloi." This humbler route leads Darrell through coal mines and cargo ships to a monastery in the Himalayas, where he learns after months of solitude that, from his point of view, the meaning of living is the achievement of spiritual rather than material gains. The only other movies I've watched as many times are *Harold and Maude*, *3 Women*, *All About Eve*, and *Valley of the Dolls*.

Clément P.J. Schneider

In the way one discovers treasures on that nebulous proposition Instagram—which means to waste as much of our waking time as possible— I found, either by suggestion or by direct message, the work of Clément P.J. Schneider. How else would I have come across the sublime portraiture of this shy, unassuming artist, which looks to me like a beautiful intersection of deeply felt expression and highly aestheticized contemporary editorial photography? So far, I see it only on Instagram. No publications beyond my own series, *Tomorrow's Man*, issues 5 and 6, have seen fit to bring this work into print. My other favorite account right now is @webuywhitealbums—conceptual pop art at its highest.

Philip Hoare
RISINGTIDEFALLINGSTAR

'Rich and strange from the tip of its title to its deep-sunk bones'
Robert Macfarlane

'A masterpiece'
Alex Preston,
Observer

RISINGTIDEFALLINGSTAR

Philip Hoare's books are a recent addition to the catalog of publications that delight me, and are rather more dense and information packed than I'm accustomed to. I've managed only two of them: *RISINGTIDEFALLINGSTAR* (2017), which is the first work of Hoare's I read, and *Albert and the Whale* (2021). The earlier book's vast stories and locales include a chapter on the Provincetown artist and former landlady of Hoare's (and of mine), Pat de Groot. Be prepared to spend a lot of time on Google; the author revels in arcane language as well as rabbit holes of topics, history, and personalities that require, on my part at least, much research.

This spread, clockwise from top left:
Bobbi Boyle, *A Day in the Life*, 1967; Philip Hoare, *RISINGTIDEFALLINGSTAR*, 2017; Nicole Canet and Florent Paudeleux, *Beautés Masculines*, 2023; Martin Scorsese and David Tedeschi, Still from *Personality Crisis*, 2022; Clément P.J. Schneider, *Nima Machado, Paris*, 2022; Edmund Goulding, Still from *The Razor's Edge*, 1946

Personality Crisis: One Night Only

Martin Scorsese and David Tedeschi's 2022 documentary *Personality Crisis: One Night Only* about, ostensibly, a swank cabaret act also functions as a master class in entertainment, storytelling, and how to become an international rock star in New York. Only Scorsese could sculpt the heroic David Johansen in such fine detail. The historical footage is breathtaking.

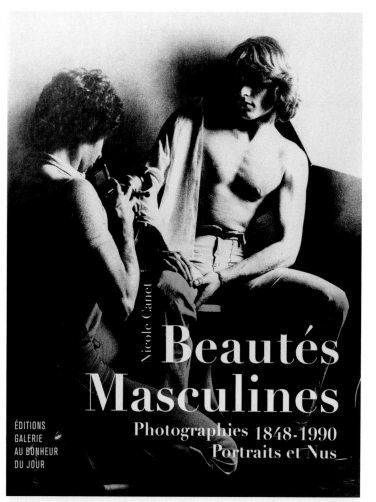

Beautés Masculines: Photographies 1848–1990, Portraits et Nus

This is the latest of Nicole Canet's exhaustively researched and handsomely designed books on European homoerotic photography. Her thirty-three others, published by her Paris gallery, Au Bonheur du Jour, many the size of doorstops, are encyclopedic paeans to their various subjects, whether male prostitution in Paris from 1860 to 1960 (*Hôtels Garnis*, 2012) or the erotic photographs of Vincenzo Galdi, assistant and model to the more well-known practitioners Guglielmo Plüschow and Wilhelm von Gloeden. Unfortunately for American rubes such as myself, they are typically not translated from the French. However, enthusiasts of this sort of material will not be disappointed.

Studio Visit

Jim Goldberg speaks with Jordan Stein about his latest book. Packed with the characters of his own life, it took him twenty-four years to make.
Photographs by Damien Maloney

"My dream was to get out of New Haven," writes Jim Goldberg in his 2017 photobook, *Candy*, a coming-of-age story that tracks his 1973 move west and the beginnings of his life as an artist, a seeker, and a man in near-constant motion. Goldberg's eye was attuned to inequality. His first book, *Rich and Poor* (1985), combined black-and-white portraits of wealthy and impoverished subjects with their hand-scrawled notes, revealing a layer of tenderness and remove in not only his newly adopted city of San Francisco but photography more broadly. *Raised by Wolves* (1995), a ten-year effort to chronicle the dizzying, often tragic lives of teenage runaways, became a cult classic book, in addition to an exhibition, using tactics that explode image and text with found and salvaged artifacts.

In the years since, evidence of the artist's existence—what he's held, literally and figuratively—has become raw material for his investigations of aging, human trafficking, transgender love, and much more. While storytellers look outward, so too do they point inward, and Goldberg's new book (though the word feels too contained, too manageable) is packed with the characters and questions of his own life.

He began the 360-page *Coming and Going* (2023) in 1999, well before its full content actually existed, like planting the seed of an unknown fruit. He had some living to do— loving, breaking up, losing his parents, and raising a daughter. Last fall, I met Goldberg at his studio north of San Francisco. We spoke about *Coming and Going*, a project twenty-four years in the making, which chronicles wild highs and dismal lows alongside the casual, nearly parenthetical moments of a life. It's a uniquely rendered autobiography told in words, pictures, and what one might best describe as suture.

Jordan Stein: **You've said that *Coming and Going* began in 1999. Is that when you started to think about it as an object, as a book?**

Jim Goldberg: Yes. At that point, I was a single dad taking care of Ruby [Goldberg's daughter]. I had collected all this stuff. I wasn't going out in the world and photographing that much. I figured I'd take this mountain, this pile of material, and try to make sense of it, and maybe it would help make sense of my own life too.

JS: **When you say you have this mountain of material, what do you mean?**

JG: I had pictures of my own life. Pictures I was taking out into the world. Collages or things that I had been doing. Pictures of my family, photos of my courtship and marriage, pictures of Ruby being born and growing up—a mountain of materials.

JS: **It took twenty-four years to make the book. Why so long?**

JG: I think life got in the way. I was a single dad, I had to make a living. I was teaching all over the place. Then I joined Magnum. So, I would work on it in fits and spurts.

JS: **How did you feel about the content of the book changing in real time with the content of your life? It's fundamentally different from 99 percent of the photobooks in the world in this regard.**

JG: It's a living organism.

JS: **How did the livingness of the thing change your thinking or your approach?**

JG: When I first did the book, it was '99, so it was really about what was immediately going on, which was marriage, birth of daughter, death of father, end of marriage, being alone, lonely for love. But as time passed, I knew I needed to modify it. As my life moved on, I organically needed to expound on it. And so I embraced that. The book dummy itself became the way for me to strategize, to work out what the story would be about. Because the story was unfolding as my book literally unfolds, in the way that I do it.

JS: **And the book dummy, we should say, is not a singular object. There are many book dummies. There's a 1999 book dummy that's the size of your fist. And then there's the most recent book dummy that you could barely fit in a suitcase.**

JG: I put it in a suitcase. It does fit.

JS: **Ha. How did it come into sharper focus?**

JG: I'm constantly mutating my ideas to find the right form. Also, like with all of my work, and certainly with my books like *Rich and Poor*, *Raised by Wolves*, even *Open See* (2009), and with *Coming and Going*, I'm trying to push the form, not just of the book but also of my documentary practice.

JS: **The epic dummy feels alive, but the finished book does too.**

JG: Well, I never thought about this, but maybe that's because it's all distilled down into the form it needed to be.

I'm constantly mutating my ideas to find the right form.

JS: **There's a lot in the book that's fairly universal, but no one else could have made this book. Tell me more about your process?**

JG: I go out in the world, slow to understand what it is I'm doing, but using my intuition I move toward putting all the pieces together. I remember things that happened in *Raised by Wolves* where it was obvious who the main characters were or what the story was, but I couldn't see it. I was still struggling with trying to find some answers, and they were right in front of my face. So, my process is bringing it back in the studio and physically playing with things, cutting and pasting and putting it into book form, and somehow the pieces of the puzzle start to fit together.

JS: **Do you think this took you longer than other projects because it's so personal? Because it was your own life?**

JG: I would imagine so. That's what I attempted to do here, to hold a mirror up to myself, and I followed the process until the story was done. I mean, maybe it could have gone on longer, but it seemed like it got to the point where it needed to be for the story, this story, to end.

JS: **Do you see this as an autobiography, as a memoir?**

JG: Now I do.

JS: **But you didn't?**

JG: Maybe I refused to see. Maybe I was naive and not seeing it, or ignorant. I felt like I had an epiphany when I was on press. It's like, Oh my God, this is an autobiography. I mean, I had been told that. I heard it. I knew it on some level.

JS: **Do you have any idea why you would have felt that on press?**

JG: Maybe because of the reality of seeing the sheets printed out. It was during the section where my mom had died. Photographs hold memories, fixed memories. Maybe it was then that the pictures came alive again, and I realized, Oh, I was telling this story. Whoa, this is really personal. Wow, this is my life.

JS: How does it feel now that it's a mass-produced object that you can hold in your hands?

JG: I'm really proud of it. It's a unique piece of work that talks about the language of photography—and words, objects, and other things—as a way to represent ideas, how to exemplify a life or how to convey a story.

JS: It's possible, also, to look at it as a giant, extraordinary collage. Is it a collage? Or does it just employ collage?

JG: I make collages and there are a lot of them in it, but I think that I see the world in a more montage-y kind of way. I'm just combining things all the time. I'm listening to you, but I also know what's going on over in the corner. I'm very watchful. I think that if I had had talent in the last century, I would have become a cubist.

JS: Because you're interested in telling a story from multiple perspectives at the same time?

JG: Yes, at the same time. Shit, that sounds conceited. I don't mean that to be pretentious.

JS: What *is* a montage? An overlapping and connecting of different scenes?

JG: [*Googling the word*] "Montage Definition. Dictionary." "The process or technique of selecting, editing, and piecing together separate sections of film to form a continuous whole. 'Montage was a useful device for overcoming the drawbacks of silent film.' A sequence of film made using the technique of montage . . . The technique of producing a new composite whole from fragments of pictures, text, or music. 'The play often verged on montage.'"

JS: I think that's what you've done.

JG: So, it is accurate.

JS: That sounds pretty accurate to me.

JG: Uh-huh. I see cinematically. So, when I design the book, I'm also thinking

of how it flows. I'm thinking of music, and that the tonality changes so that it keeps you awake, but also that it flows quickly enough so that you can embrace the story but at the same time move through it.

JS: **The cover is a literal collage, hundreds of hand-cut photographs taped together.**

JG: The front cover is two separate collages put together. The black-and-white images are the work I was making photographically at the time. The color is of my personal life, both put together. The last pages of the book and the back cover are the pictures of my life and my work now merged together. It begins as a close-up of my studio wall, and then it just zooms out again and again. Which also talks about the volume of memories, too, and things being fixed in memories—this is a book that fixes that.

JS: **It's totally cinematic. Over the course of the last several pages, it zooms out and zooms out, and you feel the weight of what a movie camera might do, and it feels overwhelming. It feels like a massive constellation of a person's life.**

JG: Right. Which refers to a few pages earlier, the constellations.

JS: **Do you want to say a quick word about what that is? There's a page that depicts the night sky.**

JG: A page of the universe. I've placed many of the most important people to me who are no longer with us and made them into stars in the universe. You just see their first names.

JS: **The story, as we might call it, the narrative maybe, begins a couple of pages in, and we're near Lima, Peru, and you let the reader (though that's not entirely the right word) know that there was a knock on your door, and you were encouraged to call your mother because your father was sick. It's telling that the story begins far from home, but you're being called back.**

JG: Coming back.

JS: **Coming back. There are a million ways to start. Why was this the right way?**

JG: I would have to look back at the old dummies to know best, because the book changed so much over time. What it is

Previous spread:
Materials for and spreads from *Coming and Going*, 2023

Opposite:
A studio shelf with pictures of Larry Sultan and Goldberg with Robert Frank, 2023
Photographs by Damien Maloney for *Aperture*

That's what I attempted to do here, to hold a mirror up to myself.

now is, basically, taking off from a book I did called *The Last Son* (2016), where the final pages are of me in a conversation with my parents on the phone. I think that they said "Good news," and the good news was that I was going to get some money from my father's disability payments. I took that money and went to Asia. Coming back from that trip, I decided I was indeed a photographer.

JS: **A few years ago, you and Alessandra [Sanguinetti] moved to a property close to where we are now, in Northern California, outside of Petaluma. Active garden. Active farm. Farm animals. Some of your time is spent with boots and gloves on, and you're out in the field doing stuff. Does that have an effect on your consciousness or your work?**

JG: Yes. It does.

JS: **It seems to me that the farm is so relevant, that there's something related to this epic process of making the book, living your life, people coming and going, vegetables, animals. . . .**

JG: The day when I decided that, You know what, I'm going to start making the pictures that are going to end the book, and I went out to do it, was the day when my friend Kelsey called and said, "There's a dead hawk in my tree. I don't know how it got here, but there's a dead hawk. You might want to take a picture of it." And I decided this was going to be the first picture that I would take to end the book. I got up on the ladder, twisted wrong, and ripped my Achilles tendon. I was out for almost a year, and I certainly had to think of my own mortality at that time. I wondered, Will the ending of the book be me "dying" and not being able to walk again?

JS: **How do you balance the undeniably heavy, life-changing moments with the regular stuff that just happens over the course of a day?**

JG: That's the most interesting part of it, those ordinary moments. That's where I feel like I've failed. Fail is not the right word. But I could have been better taking more of those prosaic moments, because those banal things that we don't think to look at all the time are really remarkable indicators of how we live.

JS: **By contrast, there's a photograph that appears to depict the moment your father dies.**

JG: Right. When my father was dying, it was Christmas morning. My mom is worried about baking cookies for the nurse's aide who is taking care of my dad. My father's dying, and my mom is worried about baking cookies. That said something about how we deal with these hard moments, sometimes by looking the other way . . . not looking at us getting a shot in the arm. Sometimes photographing is a way to distance oneself, because I'm behind the camera looking in, and I'm not seeing the intensity of the situation in the same way as if I were without the camera.

JS: It's clear at some point in the book that you're not just collecting experiences, collecting images, you're also collecting hair from haircuts and your daughter's toothbrushes. When that material appears, it's a real window into your life as someone who saves things.

JG: I've been collecting objects and exhibiting them for a long time. Because I was a single dad, the toothbrushes became these markers of time—that she would move from a Tweety toothbrush, to something a little larger, and on and on.

I think when my father died I started turning gray. And when my mom died, in 2000, is when I had to reconcile that I'm a bit more alone in the world. I'm holding on to the memories with the pictures that I've made of them or other experiences. My hair was a physical thing to record time, how I, then, was part of this cycle of . . . a marker of time.

JS: This studio full of stuff—it's almost like a laboratory. What's a day like in here?

JG: I love being here. Making things takes me out of something that happened that day—an upsetting conversation, or news of the world, et cetera. On some level, I'm a frustrated sculptor, trying to build things more three-dimensional. My being here is my attempt at doing that. The physicality of the book, and having to turn the pages, and paste, to tape together— that is heaven to me, and I haven't run out of ideas yet.

Jordan Stein is a curator and the author of *Miyoko Ito: Heart of Hearts* (2024).

Abdo Shanan, Wall
memorial for Algeria's
war of independence,
Algiers, 2023
Courtesy the artist
(See page 96)

Counter Histories

What could an archive of the future look like? What creative possibilities are offered by the gaps, absences, and silences in historical records? How can artists engage with histories that weren't photographed? How can found images contribute to a fuller understanding of the past, present, and future?

These are some of the questions that were proposed by Magnum Foundation, our partners for this issue, informed by their ongoing Counter Histories grant initiative, which supports projects that creatively reframe the past to engage with urgent questions of the present. Here, a broad range of artists contribute stories that meld the personal and the political, through both archival research and original photography.

Working in Hong Kong, Billy H.C. Kwok collaborates with a grieving mother who for years has been desperately searching for her son. In Nepal, Prasiit Sthapit investigates the complex role of musicians—as both instigators and healers—in the Maoist insurrection that shook the country for a decade. Alice Proujansky looks at her parents' past as New Left activists in the United States, while Christopher Gregory-Rivera examines how Puerto Rican independence activists were surveilled for decades. And, in the years before Poland ousted a right-wing government last fall, Agata Szymanska-Medina exposed how a nationalist party worked steadily to undermine an independent judiciary.

Family and community are as essential here as politics and memory. Stories of migration from Haiti to Philadelphia inspire Naomieh Jovin's vibrant collages, in which she seeks to honor her elders, in particular her mother. Cédrine Scheidig also engages with legacies of the Black diaspora, tracing her relationship to Afro-Caribbean history and community through regal, atmospheric portraits made in French Guiana. In the Eastern Cape of South Africa, Lindokuhle Sobekwa pays homage to his artistic forebears as he comes to terms with painful moments in his family history. He reflects on the movement of Black migrant labor and builds what he describes as a "family tree" of the country.

The photographers in Counter Histories find the gaps in image records and create their own narratives in response. Abdo Shanan, working in Algeria, looks at how the country's independence martyrs have dominated public iconography, but ordinary citizens remain unheralded. Influenced by Mahieddine Moussaoui, the Algerian independence activist and proponent of Pan-African culture, Shanan crowdsourced family pictures from friends, and made new images on the streets of Algiers, in an effort to build a speculative archive for his own generation. "A people without history is not a people," Moussaoui once said. "A country without archives is not a country." —**The Editors**

For So Many Years When I Close My Eyes

When Yu Lai Wai-ling's son disappeared from Hong Kong into China, she embarked on a tireless investigation to find him. The photographer Billy H.C. Kwok has assembled an archive related to her search—piecing together a twisting story of grief and resolve.
Ken Chen

The mother's quest began on August 24, 2000. Her name was Yu Lai Wai-ling, a housewife who lived in a public-housing estate with her husband, a civil servant, and her son, an autistic teenager. Outside the walls of their small flat, a typhoon breached Hong Kong and calmed into a storm. The unsettling weather disturbed her son, so her husband suggested a diversion: lunch. After leaving a dim sum restaurant, the three huddled through the Yau Ma Tei underground station—and this was when the boy let go of her hand, sprinted into the crowd, and disappeared.

Ms. Yu was frantic. Her son, named Yu Man-hon, was a two-year-old in a fifteen-year-old's lanky body. He couldn't speak. How could he manage the packed underground station alone? She went to the police, whose website still displays a missing person photograph of her son: a thin boy, his eyes set slightly apart, his mouth drooping. Man-hon began a journey whose mysterious sequence we can reconstruct from a Hong Kong Immigration Department report released after his disappearance. After somehow traveling twelve miles north, he inexplicably appeared behind the Chinese border at 1:47 PM, despite lacking the permit needed to cross. At the Lo Wu border checkpoint in Shenzhen, Chinese immigration officials found the boy answered to Cantonese, not Mandarin, and returned him to Hong Kong.

Immigration officials there noted the boy's disheveled state. He wore shoes from a Chinese brand. He didn't respond when they asked him about Andy Lau, one of Hong Kong's most famous celebrities. Panicking, the boy flailed his arms and spat at the officers, who handcuffed him to a chair. To them, he was clearly an "illegal" migrant. His poverty, the officers inferred, suggested a Chinese, rather than Hong Kong, origin, so they dragged him back into Shenzhen. That fateful last act separated Ms. Yu from her son.

In the coming days, Ms. Yu's tearful, inconsolable cries circulated across the newspapers and TV news. A massive force of Hong Kong police officers flooded the city. Search teams scoured Shenzhen and Guangdong. Was Man-hon still alive? Had gangsters captured him? Did he become another unhoused migrant in China? The boy came to represent Hong Kong itself—a phantom languishing inside the foreign motherland that had absorbed the former British colony only three years prior.

Billy H.C. Kwok heard about Ms. Yu and her son when he was a secondary-school student in Hong Kong. Be careful at the border, his mother had told him. Now a boy not much older than him had vanished into China. Living today between Hong Kong and Taiwan, Kwok works as a photojournalist; his images for the *New York Times* and the *Wall Street Journal* depict the contentious new Sinophone century: a Hong Kong protestor raises a flaming stick at riot police, steelworkers protest in Guangzhou, and a man fixes a flagpole outside a Taiwanese temple he's taken over with Chinese flags. In the National Archives of Taiwan, Kwok uncovered letters written by those captured and later executed during the White Terror, the authoritarian wave of oppression that began in 1947. The letters were never delivered, until Kwok intervened to complete the correspondence. For his project *Last Letters* (2017–ongoing), he approached their authors' families and photographed those who agreed to read them. The most fascinating part, Kwok told me, was observing the children of these victims kowtowing before statues of Chiang Kai-shek, the right-wing leader who presided over the persecution, only to gradually realize he had authored their own family tragedies. Kwok appreciated how these statues, whose removal he also documents, constituted both objects and manifestations of political ideology. Having made this archival interrogation into one alternative China, a project oriented less around visuality than the failure and persistence of ideological narratives within objects, Kwok wondered how he could investigate the story of Hong Kong.

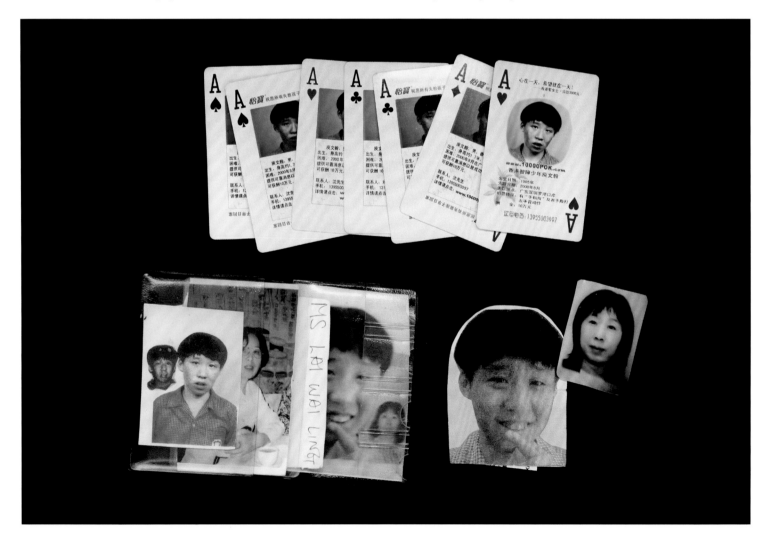

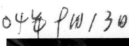

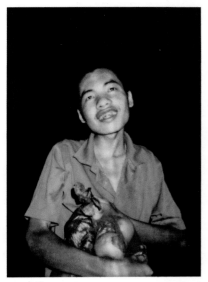

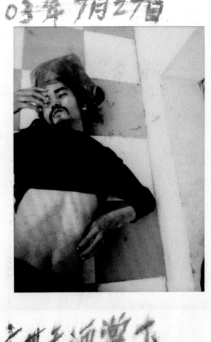

04年P내130

03年 7月27日

9.6/日 茂名市河源珠矶桥

东莞大翔大井头市场

广州天河棠下

1.主角约18岁 ② 左右

2002年 25/12

04年P내P내

1/9 茂名市河西

翁源县官渡开发区

东莞大翔毛坎市场侧

Page 35:
Billy H.C. Kwok, Installation view of *For So Many Years When I Close My Eyes* at Jockey Club Creative Arts Centre, Hong Kong, 2023

This page:
Polaroid images taken by Ms. Yu in southern Chinese cities, ca. 2000–2005; opposite: Playing cards and a transparent wallet made by Ms. Yu featuring Man-hon's portrait, ca. 2000–2003

He recalled that lost boy he'd heard about growing up, whose story hinted at a surreptitious way to interrogate Hong Kong's vexed status without triggering Chinese censorship. In June 2022, Kwok cold-called Ms. Yu, whose number he found in one of the many classified advertisements she'd placed looking for her son decades earlier. When he introduced himself as someone researching Man-hon, Ms. Yu told him to read the internet and the newspapers. I've read all the newspapers and the internet, he told her. You're the only source. He plied Ms. Yu to meet him at a restaurant, where he encountered a woman he described as deeply saddened and driven by love and discipline. By their third meeting, she invited him to her apartment.

Kwok lived only two stations away, and he visited her every week for nine months, each time carrying his camera to acclimate her to the idea of perhaps one day being photographed. However, the photographs they focused on were not his, but hers. For one

The boy came to represent Hong Kong itself—a phantom languishing inside the foreign motherland.

astonishing consequence of Ms. Yu's son's disappearance is how her search led her to deploy many of the techniques of art practice, such as object making, photography, and performance. Kwok's ongoing project has been to curate and present her archive related to her son's disappearance, and his initial instantiation, *For So Many Years When I Close My Eyes* (2022–23), combines elements of her images and records with his own maps and photographs created in locations related to her story.

Few forces in the universe are as powerful as a mother's grief. Supported by donations from people who'd heard about her loss, Ms. Yu began creating notices asking if anyone had seen Man-hon. This media project included newspaper classified ads, text-based spots aired on TV and Hong Kong trains, and, remarkably, playing cards featuring Man-hon's portrait. This collision of public memory and a simple deck of cards reminded Kwok of how the US military trained the soldiers invading Iraq to identify Saddam Hussein's leadership circle by printing their faces on playing cards. Ms. Yu also posted missing person flyers in Shenzhen and elsewhere in southern China. A few of the flyers resemble zines or print art. Monochromatic enigmas, they show her son's missing person photograph, an embellished image of him with long hair, and only the Chinese words *missing person*.

During these visits, she searched for Man-hon among the transient and disabled men she encountered. As Kwok explained to me, she would see an unhoused man, approach him, and, like some early Christian saint, brush the hair from his face. After verifying the man wasn't Han'er (her son Han, in Chinese), she would take his portrait. The resulting Polaroids include, in her handwriting, the man's name, the location, and the date. Your eyes fall upon the men's shoulders, shrunken from hunger. Their necks seem too slender, their heads and often matted, overgrown hair loom over their torsos, grown tiny from want. Another man, smiling, looks comparatively nourished. His shirt and trousers are blemished with stains. His toes jut from his right boot.

"By photographing individuals who were not Man-hon, she was able to indirectly prove his existence through some method of elimination," Kwok writes. However, these portraits did not prove he was living. They transferred his identity onto a substitute object, another man who might temporarily have contained the possibility of being Man-hon. Each portrait depicts someone not there, a vicarious memento mori. Her portraiture resembles few others because of her almost random relationship to those she photographed. Unlike a social reformer such as Jacob Riis, Ms. Yu had no investment in uplifting their plight. Their identities were almost incidental to her project, yet she documented them compulsively. Her unstudied repetition, obsessive seriality, and endless male subjects all recall efforts to index a specific population, but her portraits are not mug shots, ID cards, or a form of surveillance. She does not seek to exercise power over the "long hairs," as Kwok called these men. Her figures look the viewer in the eye without any sense of shame, but also lack the inverted grandeur that suffuses, say, Dorothea Lange's *Migrant Mother* (1936). Her Polaroids sometimes present young men roaming the nocturnal city, a genre whose closest Western correlative might be bohemian nightlife photographs, though the men here seem trapped in far more destitute straits.

Having systematically "cleared" one area, as Kwok put it, Ms. Yu went to the next. She began in Shenzhen with her husband, then gradually traveled alone through the provinces of Fujian, Jiangxi, Guangxi, and Hunan, miles inland. One Polaroid isolates Mao's famous slogan on a public building: "Serve the people." The phrase can't help but come off as charged, but Kwok describes Ms. Yu as "not really into political things." Her portraits of the poor are only a by-product of her quest—but they hint at the underbelly of the Chinese economic paradox. No other country has lifted more

Studio photographs sent
to Ms. Yu by strangers
claiming the young men
pictured were Man-hon,
ca. 2000–2010

people from poverty, yet China's manufacturing boom relied on
rural workers' moving to urban factories and forfeiting their "iron
rice bowl" of social benefits for a precarious life of contract labor.
Tens of millions lost their jobs when state-owned enterprises in
places such as Shenzhen conducted mass layoffs so that China
could enter the World Trade Organization in 2001. Left behind was
a generation of lost men—the Chinese lumpenproletariat profiled
in Ms. Yu's accidental visual ethnography. While unmotivated by
anything as idealistic as transnational solidarity, she bridged the
two Chinas—the declining former British financial center from
which she ventured and the rising superpower that absorbed it—
and created a point of contact between the lower classes of both.

狼狽風情

From either side of this border came grifters, hustlers, and con men. Fortune tellers claimed they could reveal her son's location, for a price. As Ms. Yu posted more flyers, she started receiving letters from mainland Chinese people who claimed they had found her son. "Seeing is believing," as one of them wrote, so her correspondents often sent a picture—a studio portrait of someone they claimed was Man-hon. None resemble him at all. The men possess too much reality, their setting too little. In one portrait, a man wearing a camouflage jacket, his hair unkempt, his feet filthy, sits inside a brightly ersatz setting: a pot of plastic flowers beside him, a painted backdrop of an enormous cartoon candle. Does he exist in reality or in a cartoon universe of exuberant kitsch? His mouth hangs open, as if he doesn't know.

In another portrait (featured on the cover of this issue), a man wears a three-piece suit and black loafers, an immaculate part in his hair. He crosses his legs next to a statue of a panting dog. Behind him stands a green Bob Ross–like painting of a European hamlet. While these portraits served as "evidence" of her son's existence, they look aggressively, haphazardly constructed, as if someone condensed the elaborate staging and dramatized backgrounds of the photographer Wang Qingsong into a tacky prom photograph starring the poorest of the poor. Man-hon's face, taken from that original missing person photo, sometimes appears photoshopped

onto the male figure, creating a portrait of a half-fictional person and a "loop," Kwok called it, back in time.

The letters asked for money. Others offered something else: speculative biographies of Man-hon's future life. "I am doing well in Northeast China, and these two kind people brought me to a doctor specializing in neurology in Harbin City, who cured my mental illness," writes one faux Man-hon in a 2005 letter. Ms. Yu tore up at least one letter. Then her innate sense of organization took over, and she taped it back together. "You never know who is in the photos," Kwok told me, but he had a guess. He noticed certain figures reappeared despite the letters' coming from different addresses, and concluded Ms. Yu's pen pals were human traffickers.

"I won't beat around the bush. I just want to help you find a brand-new son," begins another. "His name is Tang Xiaolong, born on April 13, 1986. . . . He will make you love him like an object." If Ms. Yu wanted to be introduced to her replacement son, another correspondent told her, she could meet him on October 20, 2003, beneath the dragon statue at Longcheng Plaza in Shenzhen, which was the first Chinese Special Economic Zone designed to attract foreign investment. When Man-hon disappeared, the city's GDP was dwarfed by its Hong Kong neighbor ($22 billion versus $171 billion), but as Shenzhen became the so-called Silicon Valley of China, the two cities swapped places economically. Ms. Yu did not show up for the meeting. Kwok himself trekked to Longcheng Plaza recently, and his gleaming but somber photograph of the dragon statue seems to evoke the city's intense gentrification and China's own triumphant self-image—a perhaps too-glossy counterpoint to Ms. Yu's raw, street-level eye. This photograph appeared in his 2023 installation at Hong Kong's Para Site art center, accompanied by his deployment of geolocation to pin down Ms. Yu's portraits of unhoused men and the studio portraits. His mapping suggested that she and her correspondents worked not far from each other, each photographing Chinese men who were not her son.

Ms. Yu created more than three hundred Polaroids and received around one hundred letters, but later made more portraits, using other cameras and her phone, not included in Kwok's project. She also says that four-fifths of the total material was stolen by a Chinese businessman who claimed he wanted to make a documentary about her. Kwok sees himself as a "researcher" or "investigator" behind a photographic practice "mostly driven by her intentions." As he told me in his Cantonese-inflected English, "She really think what photography is." Inverting the usual gendered division of art, she captured men living on the streets, while he photographed the domestic space of her apartment, her five rooster figurines peering out her window, their cries meant to scare off ominous spirits during Chinese funerals.

One day, Ms. Yu asked Kwok if he would create her portrait. She told him where to set up the camera and where she would sit. Just before Kwok clicked the shutter, she closed her eyes. When he asked why, Ms. Yu responded, "Photography is capturing a happiness moment." Every day, she explained, she closes her eyes and dreams of her son. After he made a print, Kwok asked her to inscribe a message for Man-hon in the negative space of the background. To his surprise, she wrote out her statement immediately, as if it was some text she already knew. These are the words I say every morning, she told him, when I gaze out the window and look for my son. The first sentence reads, "Han'er, whom I miss day and night, are you still safe?"

Ken Chen teaches at Barnard College.
He is the author of the poetry collection
Juvenilia (2010).

致 翰兒

　　我朝夕念掛的翰兒，你還安在嗎？是母親的生命之舟把你帶來這世界，原本以為在我們這個平凡平靜的家中一家人可以平安愉快地生活，過安穩溫馨的日子。

　　自從2000年8月24日中午11：20我們母子在地鐵站失散後，你被香港入境處人員錯誤地強行遣送到深圳以至在內地失蹤。從此改變了翰兒你的命運，也改變了我們家的一切。沒有你的日子，原本暖暖的充滿笑聲的家變得冷冷的甚是淒清，母親我從此被困在無底的痛苦之淵。

翰兒啊，你這羔羊被強迫離群的孤雁到底在哪裡？父母和親友們踏破鐵鞋走遍南北東西就是不見你的蹤影。卓翰兒啊，餓了你吃甚麼？冷了有衣嗎？病了怎麼辦？你可否聽到母親悲切的呼喚？

兒，千萬記住快回來吧我的翰你回到母親請求有心人幫助會繼續努力尋身邊來，母親將找你。

　　懸念翰兒愁緒如麻無處問生死，引頸以待五中盡裂，疲憊不堪的殘軀百病叢生遠往難，母親拜托清風捎去我的祝福。祝卓翰兒平安慈早歸家。倘若你已離開這世界，記住要托夢告訴母親你在天國是否安好，母親會祈求神佑你安康快樂，來生我們再續母子之緣，到那時我們會共享有平安健康幸福快樂！

母親泣字
二零二二年十月八日

Lindokuhle Sobekwa
The Country

Kwanele Sosibo

A vast and variegated holiday destination, a bottomless repository of cheap Black labor, and a site of bitterly fought wars of resistance against colonial dispossession—South Africa's Eastern Cape is as beautiful as it is unknowable. The province occupies the moodiest quarter of the country's coastline and stretches into the semiarid escarpment and the southern edge of the Drakensberg mountain range. Its landscape is at parts lush, rugged, pristine, and broken.

In the Johannesburg-based photographer Lindokuhle Sobekwa's newest series *Ezilalini (The Country)* (2020–ongoing), the elements guide a search for wholeness. The terrain—misty, parched, and undulating—offers more vestiges and apparitions than signposts. Sobekwa likens the segue into this project, in which he travels between the township of Thokoza, where he grew up, and his parents' rural homesteads, to "digging a hole I'm afraid to look into." This outsiderness is writ large over many of the photographs. It is visible in the scraps of land overused to the point of collapse, in the somnambulism of everyday routines that overburden women, and in an idleness in young men interrupted only by the gendered enactment of ceremonial roles.

Sobekwa began making frequent trips to the Eastern Cape for an earlier series on the troubled life of his late elder sister. Even as he mapped his family tree, an endeavor to which he gives repetitious, totemic expression throughout *Ezilalini*, his obsession was undergirded by a desire to think of home in less regimented ways. "It's not only about my family, it's a family tree about South Africa," he explains. "The history, the migration, my family's legacy with mines. I almost worked in the mines myself. A lot of people can relate to that."

Trees, plant life, and graves anchor this trip through the countryside. One of the project's more evocative images, made in Tsomo, depicts his mother, shoulders covered and back to the camera, paying respects to her daughter and brother. Her reverence, split between two graves, recalls Sobekwa's struggle to reconcile the maternal and paternal branches of his family tree.

Sobekwa was introduced to photography through Of Soul and Joy, a workshop in Johannesburg's East Rand, in 2012, as a high school student. Given the speed at which he developed his talents, Sobekwa's dilemma would be honing a personal style from the wide pool of influences at his disposal. "My early work says a lot about the people that inspired me, like Ernest Cole, Santu Mofokeng, Peter Magubane, David Goldblatt," he states. "I'm lucky that I discovered that passion early on, and I took it seriously."

He remembers being reduced to tears on his first encounter with Cole's 1967 photobook *House of Bondage*, and his ego being shattered by Mofokeng, who simply told Sobekwa to read in order to frame his work on his own terms. Sobekwa's oeuvre is fittingly laden with homage. But the vulnerability with which he approaches his subject matter reveals a generational encumberment—a fitful, perhaps sacrificial, desire to get to grips with the cumulative horrors of a society coming undone. In this pursuit, the twenty-eight-year-old Sobekwa has turned to both the rich canon of his home country and the work of others who have continued to challenge the constraints of documentary photography. The power of a work like *Ezilalini* is that it provides the space for both personal contemplation and the difficult, wider political reflection required in a nation as young as South Africa.

Sobekwa's work provides the space for personal contemplation and the wider political reflection required in a nation as young as South Africa.

Viewing the series, we flit between Tsomo, his mother's homestead, and Qumbu, 120 miles northeast, where his father was raised. Each location holds sacred family folklore: how his grandmother went into labor on a hilly outcrop in Tsomo, earning his mother the name Nontaba, meaning "child of the mountain."

In all these images, Sobekwa invites the harshness of rural life to stare at us in poetic ways, even as some of his subjects avert their gazes. The posed images do not mask the tensions, both personal and societal, arising in the wake of his search. In one image made in Qumbu, a church in which Sobekwa's father married his first wife stands gutted after a fire. In another, Sobekwa photographs a woman named Gogo Lucy Zwane as she inhales the scent of hollyhocks from a garden she planted as a symbol of peace, as apartheid's secret agents fueled political violence. On the same ground where photojournalists once recorded grim scenes, Sobekwa authors a new myth, one that recasts the killing fields of Thokoza as dreamy, fragile panoramas of serenity.

Kwanele Sosibo is a writer based in Berkeley.

Previous spread:
Women carry stacks
of wood for *umgidi*, a
traditional ceremony to
celebrate boys' coming
back from the mountains
for initiation school,
Qumbu, Eastern Cape,
2020

This page:
Newly graduated initiates
from Qumbu Black Hill
village, Eastern Cape,
2021; following spread:
Sobekwa's mother visiting
the family's ancestral
graveyard, Tsomo, Eastern
Cape, 2020

Sobekwa's father's
childhood friends from
Ntabasigogo village,
Qumbu, Eastern Cape,
2020

Sobekwa's aunt in
Ekhwenzane village,
where his maternal family
lives, Tsomo, Eastern
Cape, 2020

A street food stall on
Khumalo Street, Thokoza,
Johannesburg, 2021

The ruins of a church where
Sobekwa's father was
married, Qumbu, Eastern
Cape, 2020

Girls from the Nala clan
during a traditional
ceremony called *intlombe*,
Cofimvaba, Eastern Cape,
2021

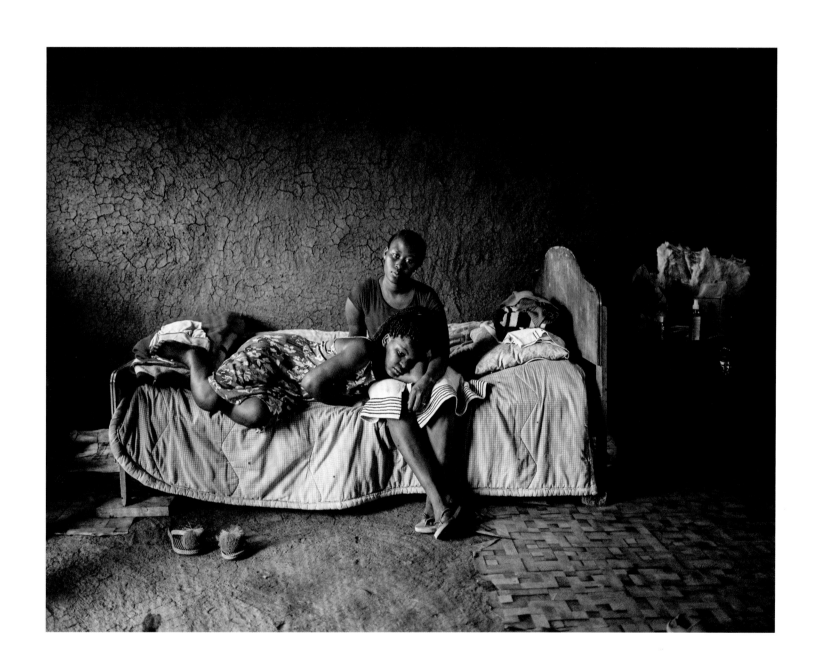

Christopher Gregory-Rivera

We See It All

For decades, US officials sought to suppress independence movements in Puerto Rico, spying on activists and their families. What do their formerly secret files reveal about this chapter of history?

Yxta Maya Murray

As a high school student in Puerto Rico, around 2005, Christopher Gregory-Rivera grew active in student movements that fought university tuition hikes. His mother wasn't happy about it. "She would say, '*Cuidado, te van a carpetear*,' which meant that the police were going to open a file on me," Gregory-Rivera told me recently. "That was my first exposure to the idea that the police were opening files, or *carpetas*, on dissidents. I was like, 'Mom's crazy, she's paranoid,' but it turned out to be something that's super present in Puerto Rican protest culture and the Puerto Rican imaginary in general."

Gregory-Rivera's mother's warnings prompted questions about his homeland, and he soon learned the violent history of *carpetas* ("folders"). Since the early 1900s, an active independence movement sought to wrest Puerto Rican sovereignty from the United States, while the Puerto Rican government and high-ranking US officials such as J. Edgar Hoover sought to suppress activists through tactics that ranged from monitoring to murder. By 1978, pressures came to a head when an undercover police agent named Alejandro González Malavé led the independence activist Arnaldo

Darío Rosado and his teenage associate Carlos Soto Arriví to Cerro Maravilla, a mountain at the center of the island. The young men allegedly planned to set fire to or bomb television towers positioned there but were met by officers who killed them in a barrage of gunfire.

The island's governor at the time, Carlos Antonio Romero Barceló, later called the police officers "heroes," in accord with the official story—that the victims had been terrorists and the police acted in self-defense. But in 1983, the Judiciary Committee of the Senate of Puerto Rico determined the youths had been executed by the police to intimidate the *independentistas*. (It also turned out that the FBI had advance knowledge of the ambush.) During the prosecutions that followed, a former agent of the Intelligence Division, William Colón Berríos, admitted the police kept files on activists. The whispered fears of being "foldered" had circulated through Puerto Rico for decades but, until that time, were often chalked up to rumor. Now people learned the stories were real. Since the 1930s, the police had investigated at least 135,000 individuals (about 3 percent of the island) suspected

SUSPENSIONES SUMARIAS

Bosque Pérez, José A.   Y2-1092

Braña Mulero, Gloria J.   N1-0757

FORTURO CANDELAS JOSE R   72-2773

Ramón Grasfoguel Bidot

López Fuentes, Linda
801-73-4267

MARTINEZ BAS PEDRO JAIME   72-4827

Pagán Hernández, Humberto
801-68-6220

801-69-8347 Santana
Rivera, Rubén

of favoring independence. Moreover, they'd used informants—suspects' associates, friends, and sometimes even family members.

These revelations gave way to litigation, and in 1988 the Puerto Rican Supreme Court declared that the police's dossier practice violated the constitutional rights to speech, association, and privacy, while also insulting "the dignity of the human being." The court required that the files be returned to their subjects, a measure the legal scholar Marc-Tizoc González describes as "habeas data." Instead of instituting a formal protocol that would help give citizens some emotional closure, people were simply told to come to the Center to Arrange Confidential Records and pick up their unredacted papers. There was no reconciliation process, no truth commission. Beginning in September 1989, people grabbed their files from the Center, took them home, read them, and then stored them in their bureaus or cupboards. If no one showed up to claim a *carpeta*, it was stored in the National Archives, where many remain today.

Twenty-four years after this process began, Gregory-Rivera was in Washington, DC, striving toward his dream of becoming a photojournalist. Posted to the White House and on Capitol Hill while working as an intern for the *New York Times*, he began to reimagine his career when he heard about Edward Snowden's 2013 data leaks, which revealed that the National Security Agency

had collected the phone records of millions of Verizon customers. "Everyone was like, 'It's not important, I have nothing to hide,'" Gregory-Rivera says. "But I knew that in Puerto Rico, everyone is afraid to express themselves politically because they think that the government is watching them. I had this crisis. So, I went back to Puerto Rico and started this project."

The project turned into a two-phase undertaking. In its first stage, Gregory-Rivera approached people in possession of their *carpetas* and asked to photograph the documents. "I did it guerrilla-style, setting up little studios in people's homes. I found the images detonated a sense of reality to a chapter of our history that a lot of people are not familiar with, especially the younger generations," he explains. The effort resulted in the series *Las Carpetas* (2014–ongoing), which shows the files as Gregory-Rivera encountered them: "A lot of people were like, 'What the hell is he doing?' when I'd bring all this equipment into their houses. But some are really proud of how big their *carpeta* is, it's as if that was a sign of their commitment to the movement."

A striking picture in *Las Carpetas* showcases a massive stack of manila files overflowing with mug shots and chillingly banal reports on the comings and goings of dissidents: one account describes a subject "seen cruising around in a green 1952 Studebaker, license plate 625-420." Others amount to loving portraits of the books confiscated from presumed *independentistas*—Kim Il Sung's biography, William J. Pomeroy's *Guerrilla Warfare and Marxism*. "The intelligence department had one of the most extensive archives of leftist literature," Gregory-Rivera tells me, wryly.

Gregory-Rivera's project gained depth and intensity when, in 2014, he began digitizing the files orphaned in the archives, including the surveillance photographs. Many of the pictures in the *carpetas* look like they could come from a family scrapbook or were ripped from refrigerator magnets, but they are actually surveillance images taken by government agents. An image, appearing to be from the 1980s, discloses two men sporting matching mustaches standing close together in fetching white shirts. Another photograph (possibly circa 1970, judging from one man's slim, striped pants) shows a woman lying on the ground, screaming with laughter, as friends try to help her up. Elsewhere, a woman in a white suit is caught in an obsessive, Eadweard Muybridge–like sequence as she opens the door of a car, takes off her blazer, and prepares to enter the vehicle. Additional evidence of the surveillance's persistence and duration surfaces in an annotated image that likely dates from the 1940s or 1950s, its five male subjects wearing natty sport coats and full-legged trousers reminiscent of midcentury zoot suits.

The surveillance photographs show an artist's flair, revealing the care with which spies conducted their craft: a smiling man, eating from a plate, leans against a telephone pole, creating a focal center of gravity with his pals arrayed behind him, grinning and hoisting signs. In a scene that tells a recognizable story of obligation and boredom, five people occupy a waiting room, watched over by what appears to be a Coppertone ad bearing the disorienting slogan "Don't Be a Paleface!" The women are carefully adorned in stockings, scarves, and curled hair, while one man smiles for the camera, his lap burdened with his and his wife's bulky coats. But the details of this event are lost to us—we don't know where the subjects are, what they are waiting for, or what happened to them when they left this space.

Gregory-Rivera collected these photographs and a cache of about sixty more, compiling them into the mesmerizing book *El Gobierno Te Odia* (The government hates you, 2023). Made on a Risograph machine, which replicates the texture of an old-fashioned Xerox copier, the tome is hand-bound with screw posts that mimic the accoutrements of what the photographer calls "office culture." For the larger part of the book, Gregory-Rivera presents the photographs with minimal identifying information in order to replicate the mystery and confusion he encountered in the National Archives. Toward the end of *El Gobierno Te Odia*, however, he appends narratives to a small selection of images.

One such picture shows a feminist activist wearing a striped hat and carrying a sign that bears the words "La violación es un acto de agresión" ("Rape is an act of aggression"). Below the image, Gregory-Rivera's text reads: "By the late 1970s and early '80s leaders of both leading parties realized they could use the Intelligence Division to control ideology beyond independence. Feminist, labor, and environmental organizations were also targeted by the secret police." We also see a photograph of a smiling woman posing before two cakes that are lavishly frosted with the letters "FUPI" (for Federación Universitaria Pro-Independencia) and "PSP" (for Partido Socialista Puertorriqueño) and planted with US flags bearing fifty-one stars, evincing the subject's ambition for Puerto Rico to become a state: "A presumed agent or employee of the Intelligence Division poses with a cake . . . decorated with frosting spelling acronyms of the various organizations the Division surveilled," Gregory-Rivera's text explains. Perhaps the most painful photographs in *El Gobierno Te Odia* are found in a diptych of Arnaldo Darío Rosado, who died at Cerro Maravilla. A 1975

Arnaldo Darío Rosado, identified with a faint number fourteen on the print, 1975

The surveillance photographs show an artist's flair, revealing the care with which spies conducted their craft.

A presumed intelligence agent poses with two cakes during a diploma ceremony at police headquarters in San Juan, 1981

portrait of the intense, bespectacled young man shows him looking at the camera while standing in a crowd of comrades; its companion image displays his bloody body lying in a field.

Gregory-Rivera's work with archives exposes surveillance's long-standing wound. Organizations and societies have betrayed their citizens in similar ways—the FBI notoriously monitored civil rights activists in the 1960s and '70s—but some have attempted to facilitate restorative justice: For former citizens of East Germany, officials made Stasi files available to the public and, in the 1990s, also convened two truth commissions that held public hearings. In 2022, Colombia's Truth Commission issued a report on that country's conflict, addressing illegal spying and lambasting US policy. Yet—as is the case with other US surveillance schemes, such as that of the Mississippi State Sovereignty Commission—there has been no collective process to address the injustice of *las carpetas*.

When I asked him whether he was trying to build a space for mourning and resolution, Gregory-Rivera affirmed that the silence surrounding *las carpetas* motivated him. "What I'm doing goes hand in hand with creating dialogue, however painful or complicated or controversial," he says. "I think these events need to be rescued because of the current political situation in Puerto Rico. This history helps us understand where we come from and to modulate for self-determination on a basic level. It can help us move into the future, and part of that process requires reconciling this history and bringing truth to the foreground on a larger scale." *Las Carpetas* and *El Gobierno Te Odia* allow the victims of surveillance, their descendants, and the United States as a whole to bear witness to a sordid chapter of history. Gregory-Rivera's work offers the opportunity for us to consider the record of political persecution and to imagine new ways of healing and moving forward.

Yxta Maya Murray is a regular contributor to *Aperture* and the author of *Art Is Everything* (2021).

Protesters on the street,
late 1970s

Christopher Gregory-Rivera, A confiscated copy of *La Crónica Gráfica* (San Juan), 1987, No. 136, 2016

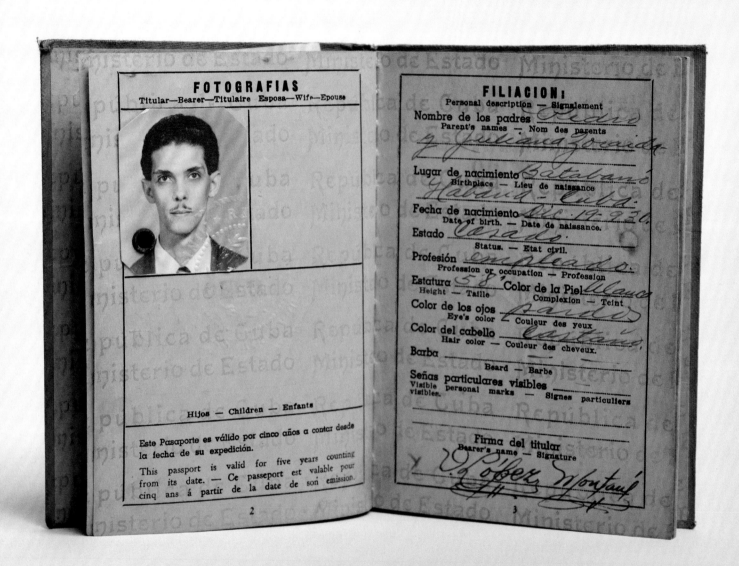

Woman after a protest at the University of Puerto Rico, 1980
Photographs by Christopher Gregory-Rivera © the artist. Archival images courtesy the Archivo General de Puerto Rico, San Juan

Moonsongs for Earth

Prasiit Sthapit

How did music propel a Maoist revolution in Nepal?
Muna Gurung

Previous spread:
Prasiit Sthapit, Pradeep
Dewan playing the
harmonium in his home,
Kathmandu, 2022

This page:
Prasiit Sthapit, The stage
for a concert by musicians,
many affiliated with the
Communist Party of Nepal
(CPN-Maoist), World Music
Day, 2022

When the People's War began in Nepal, in 1996, eight-year-old Prasiit Sthapit noticed that his great-grandfather's portrait had suddenly disappeared from the living-room wall. Later, as an adult, he realized that the picture of the mustachioed man he had assumed to be his great-grandfather was, in fact, a framed poster of Joseph Stalin. Sthapit's grandfather, an ardent Communist, looked up to Stalin. In the decade-long, violent armed conflict between the Communist Party of Nepal (CPN-Maoist) and the state, anyone left-leaning was seen as a Maoist sympathizer, and many were arrested or, worse, disappeared. During Sthapit's teen years, his family's political leanings, as well as his own youthful romanticization of what a revolution symbolizes, made him curious about the bloody rebellion that shook Nepal.

His interest in this history deepened in 2006 when, at age eighteen, he took a spontaneous trip with friends, a month after the war had ended, through the western Nepali districts of Rukum and Rolpa—the heartland of the revolution. These areas had been a war zone just weeks before. "We saw bullet holes on bridges and houses. I met many Maoists; some were curious and kind, others not so much. I realized how sheltered we were in Kathmandu, and how the war was not over in the minds and lives of many people," Sthapit told me over coffee one morning last fall in Kathmandu. Many in the capital initially experienced the war as something that would never reach them—just some hooligans making noise with pressure-cooker bombs that would surely die down in no time.

A section of the cultural wing of the Maoist party, Salyan, late 1990s
Courtesy Mohit Shrestha Collection

But the war lasted ten years, and in that time, many brothers, sisters, friends, and relatives, fighting on opposing sides—with the Maoist-led People's Liberation Army (PLA) or the Nepal Police—brutally killed one another. When the war ended, at least thirteen thousand Nepali men, women, and children had been killed, thirteen hundred disappeared, and thousands were left displaced and disabled. Although the war started in February 1996, the seeds of the revolt had been sown back in the 1960s. At the time, Nepal was brought under Panchayat rule, wherein the country's leader, King Mahendra, instated an autocratic regime that saw the dissolution of parliamentary democracy, a ban on political parties, the imprisonment and exile of elected leaders, and the curtailment of freedom of expression and many civil rights. The Panchayat era was notorious also for instituting the erasure of the country's diverse peoples, cultures, and languages under the slogan "one king, one nation, one language, one costume." It was under this system that many Maoist leaders, then in their twenties, became radicalized.

Inspired by Peru's far-left group Sendero Luminoso (Shining Path), the Maoists waged guerrilla warfare, attacking police stations, acquiring weapons, using different aliases while living and working underground among the people, and recruiting new members through song, speeches, and stories. They gained momentum and support in the rural areas of western and midwestern Nepal. As the war progressed, news of casualties increased. Reports of bomb blasts became frequent. In 2001, the government declared a state of emergency. Even urban areas such as Kathmandu saw army patrols and barbed-wire checkpoints. Freedom of expression, movement, and assembly were curtailed; state crackdowns and raids in search of Maoists increased, as did countrywide shutdowns and curfews. The government declared the Maoists "terrorists," violent revolutionaries whose image—

The music was medicine, a balm, and also a reminder for fighters who were alive to continue the mission of building a just world.

Prasiit Sthapit, Jhankar
Budha Magar with his
sarangi, Chunbang,
Rukum, 2020

in camouflage, a red bandana with a star tied across the forehead,
guns in hand—became feared.

It is this one-dimensional view that Sthapit complicates in
his project *Moonsongs for Earth* (2022–ongoing), a studied look
at the musicians who energized the Maoist movement through
song. "There was the PLA, who carried guns and bombs, and
then there were musicians, who carried guitars and harmoniums,"
Sthapit said as he scrolled through images from the series,
which includes a mix of his own contemporary portraits, archival
imagery, videos, interviews, and songs. Many of the archival
photographs feature musicians posing in nature with their
instruments, showing the world what they love and how they
want to be seen. Group photographs depict them practicing
and performing. "We had seen plenty of war images in the media,
but I wanted to see the war through the eyes of the musicians,"
Sthapit explained. "These intimate musical sessions too were

a part of the war. These musicians held and spread the dream of the revolution through their songs."

In 2019, Sthapit traveled to what is marketed as the Guerrilla Trail, a path the PLA used during the war that cuts across the spine of the country and branches out like a tree. He initially had begun working on a multimedia project to uncover stories of the war along the trail, until he met the former Maoist Jhankar Budha Magar, who sang for Sthapit a popular war song: "You must fight and win this final battle. Torn hearts and drenched bodies are waiting for a new day." The song is part of an opera, *Returning from the Battlefield*, by the late Khusiram Pakhrin, a musician and cultural leader of the revolution. The opera was commissioned for the 2005 central committee meeting of the Maoist party in the village of Chunbang. This meeting would prove historic, as it opened a path for two feuding Maoist leaders—Pushpa Kamal Dahal and Baburam Bhattarai—to reconcile their differences. A video from the gathering captures the two visibly sobbing as they watch the opera, which presents the story of a soldier's death, his willingness to sacrifice himself for the larger cause, and his wife's plea to continue fighting to fulfill the dream of the revolution. The Chunbang meeting would be followed by the formation of an antimonarchy alliance with mainstream political parties and a 2006 peace accord marking the end of the war. In 2006, the second People's Movement began, and by 2008, the country's 240-year-old monarchy was brought to an end. The new, secular Federal Democratic Republic of Nepal was born, with the Maoist party elected to office. Dahal became the republic's first prime minister. Since then, the Maoists have come into power four times, and Dahal is currently the country's prime minister.

Would the outcome in Chunbang have been different had there been no musicians, no opera, no tears? "Our duty was to sing encouraging farewell songs to our friends going into battle," the musician Laxmi Gurung told Sthapit during an interview from her home in Kathmandu. In 1999, the twenty-two-year-old Gurung joined the Maoist party after the state killed her father. "Everyone used to think of me as the daughter of a Maoist who would amount to nothing. I didn't join the party only for revenge, but I wanted to show that I could change the world and make it beautiful," she said. Later, Gurung lost her daughter during the conflict. And it has been more than twenty-four years since her husband went missing. Today, Gurung, now forty-six, doesn't want violence: "If there has to be another war again, I hope it will be a war led by love, and a war where we fight with our ideas to change society, not guns and bombs." During their conversation, she broke into a popular war song: "In the battlefield, my friend, in the battlefield. The lives of the brave will flower in the battlefield." Midway through, she stopped singing and let out a sharp laugh. "How can life flower if you're dead? But that song would get everyone riled up. Everyone would be ready to kill, ready to give their lives."

The musician and educator Pradeep Dewan, who calls himself "the people's artist," described music as the salt of the revolution. Like many Maoist musicians, Dewan was influenced by the progressive songs of the 1960s and '70s, most composed by left-leaning Nepali writers and musicians whose lyrics brought people to the streets to protest against Panchayat rule. But even with a movement toward democracy in the early 1990s, Dewan saw little change. "Everyone had a feudal mindset that they couldn't seem to shake," he explained to Sthapit. In 1997, Dewan joined the Maoists. Like many on the movement's cultural front, he traveled around the nation, training other musicians and convincing people to "walk the path of revolution." They wrote and performed hundreds of songs to excite, educate, and capture the hearts and minds of various oppressed groups: the poor, women, Dalits, and farmers.

The musicians were also healers. After battles, they sang songs to not only memorialize the dead but console their families and

Top:
Prasiit Sthapit, Magar's sarangi, Chunbang, Rukum, 2020

Bottom:
Magar, Mohit Shrestha, and others performing during People's Liberation Army training, Ot, Rolpa, 2000
Courtesy Mohit Shrestha Collection

Opposite:
Prasiit Sthapit, Laxmi
Gurung at her apartment,
Kathmandu, 2022

This page, top:
Gurung in her performance
uniform, Solukhumbu,
2003; bottom: Gurung at
age twenty-two, when she
had just joined the party,
Sindhuli, 1999
Courtesy Laxmi Gurung
Collection

friends, as well as the many who were wounded. The music was medicine, a balm, and also a reminder for fighters who were alive to continue the mission of building a just world. Today, some musicians express frustration that the goals of the revolution—equality across caste and class lines, health care, good schools, security—were never fully realized. The popular musician and writer Mohit Shrestha expressed anger and betrayal. "I've thrown away all my diaries with lyrics and unrecorded songs. They did not feel important. I didn't know that someone like you would come looking for them one day," he told Sthapit. "These songs painted a dream of a revolution, but they didn't bring the change we wanted."

Moonsongs for Earth not only shows us a different aspect of the war but also illustrates what hope can look and sound like. "I am not trying to glorify war," Sthapit told me. "The war was not only gruesome, it was a disastrous failure in many ways, but I think the motivation behind any revolution has to be considered. These artists, these humans, really believed that their singing and their music would bring change not only to Nepal but to the entire world." Today, many of them are invited to perform original and cover songs on radio or television, or they find audiences on social media and YouTube. While some are still affiliated with the Maoist party, others have moved away from politics altogether.

As an image maker and a storyteller, Sthapit is an expert at revealing and concealing, nudging viewers to understand that things are not always as they appear. When I asked what surprised him most while making *Moonsongs for Earth*, he said that it was Laxmi Gurung's vulnerability. He hadn't expected a "steely Maoist fighter" to be this soft. "She thinks there is no one in the world who cries as much as she does," he explained. "During the war, she would go into the forest, or lock herself in her room, and just cry. Even today, she cries when she composes music. Everything touches her."

Muna Gurung is a writer, translator, and educator based in Kathmandu, Nepal.

Top:
Prasiit Sthapit, Mahesh
Arohee at home, Ghorahi,
Dang, 2023; bottom:
Prasiit Sthapit, Arohee's
diary with his songs,
Ghorahi, Dang, 2023

Top:
Arohee (right) and
comrade Ritesh, both from
Magarat Cultural Family,
clad in combat gear, Palpa,
2004
Courtesy Mahesh Arohee
Collection

Bottom:
Prasiit Sthapit, Arohee's
room with a photograph of
him taken during the war,
Ghorahi, Dang, 2023

Top:
Prasiit Sthapit, Shrestha's harmonium and diary of songs, Kathmandu, 2022

Bottom, left:
Shrestha (right) with a friend, ca. 2000; right: Shrestha during a training session for new musicians of the party, Arkha, Pyuthan, 2002
Courtesy Mohit Shrestha Collection

Like the writers Frantz Fanon, Aimé Césaire, and Édouard Glissant before her, Cédrine Scheidig is, to borrow the words of Glissant's American translator, a distinguished theorist of "Caribbean self-formation." Born in 1994 in the Seine-Saint-Denis suburbs northeast of Paris to a French mother and a Guadeloupean father, Scheidig began taking photographs in her early twenties. Her first mature work explored the immigrant communities in which she grew up. Her father had left Guadeloupe in the 1970s, one of many young men drawn from the Caribbean to European capitals such as London and Paris by the promise of employment and economic prosperity.

While studying in Arles, a city in southern France renowned for its art school and photography festival, Scheidig established a deliberately time-consuming, labor-intensive practice—bulky camera equipment, analog film, handmade prints—to undercut some of the more damning associations of photography as a gendered discourse and an ethnographic tool. In plain terms, this gave her multiple ways of relating to people in the process of taking their pictures. Scheidig describes photography in general as a language, and in particular as the most textured, tactile, and best language for critically engaging the world around her.

Over the past five years, Scheidig has developed an expansive body of work on the experience of Blackness in forging both regional and diasporic Afro-Caribbean identities. She has photographed young men popping wheelies in the Martinican capital, Fort-de-France, and delved into the riotous world of carnival sound systems in London's Notting Hill. Moving nimbly from Europe to Africa, the Antilles, and Latin America, she followed tenuous but meaningful connections among young people who recognize themselves in one another despite being geographically scattered. These connections emerge through music, fashion, and hip-hop culture, which coexist in Scheidig's photographs alongside hints of ceremonial magic, overabundant nature, and a protectively vague sense of spiritualism. True to Glissant's playfulness with language and his insistence on associative thinking, Scheidig's photography expresses all these elements in a barrage of arresting details. Her portraits, landscapes, and still lifes deliver alternating jolts of familiarity and strangeness as she brings objects together in unexpected combinations.

The strength of Scheidig's most recent series, *This trace where salt was* (2023), dwells in the deceptive simplicities of a worn-out blue-and-white tiled floor, a Brooklyn Nets jersey, and three incongruous sets of angels' wings. Each photograph is keyed to a larger set of historical circumstances as Scheidig attends to the specificities of hair, scarring, tattoos, bejeweled hands, and bursts of self-fashioning, as evidenced by her striking portrait of a defiant young woman, set against the murky coast of French Guiana, with a dramatic line of safety pins running down and holding together the front of her dragon-adorned crop top.

This trace where salt was grew out of a five-week residency in the French Guianese capital, Cayenne, a city marked by French colonial history, the brutalities of the transatlantic slave trade, proximity to the Caribbean (and what Glissant termed *créolité*), and the survival of several Amerindian and Amazonian Indigenous communities. The residency program, called Foto Kontré, was designed as an exchange among artists from Guadeloupe, Martinique, and French Guiana, three territories that to this day share the twenty-first-century weirdness of being overseas departments of France, having never won independence and therefore having never decolonized.

Through the photographs she produced in Cayenne, Scheidig triangulates France, the Caribbean, and the South American continent just as she reconfigures the relationship of the horizon, the ocean, and the coast, or the city, the density of the forest, and the suggestion of a spirit world. Scheidig describes *This trace where salt was* as both a part of her engagement with the Caribbean and a mechanism for loosening and extending that project. "I'm not working in closed circles," she says. The series pushes her work beyond notions of islands or identities alone to consider more complicated but ultimately more productive (and more productively Glissantian) sites of encounter, collision, and entanglement.

Cédrine Scheidig
Searching for Cayenne

Kaelen Wilson-Goldie

Kaelen Wilson-Goldie is a writer based in Geneva and Beirut.

Agata Szymanska-Medina

The "Good" Change

Camila McHugh

A gray-haired woman looks upward intently, her gaze fixed, head tilted back, and face mask lowered to amplify her shout—a picture of defiance. Taken by the Polish artist and photojournalist Agata Szymanska-Medina, it's among the striking portraits in her recent series *"Dobra" Zmiana*, or *The "Good" Change* (2020–23), which investigates the erosion of democracy in Poland since the nationalist Law and Justice Party (PiS) came to power in 2015. Her photograph shows one of the demonstrators who since 2016 gathered in front of the state television channel (TVP 1) headquarters in Warsaw every evening during the prime-time news to protest the station's daily propaganda. The image is emblematic of Szymanska-Medina's project—she aims to bring clarity to the stories of people at the peripheries of official power.

Before PiS was removed from power as a result of the October 15, 2023, elections—an outcome that echoes the significance of Poland's 1989 elections, which led to the peaceful end of decades of stringent communism—the party had assaulted LGBTQ rights, violently rejected refugees at the Belarusian border, and by way of a constitutional tribunal in 2020 instituted a near-total ban on abortion. The latter was met with monthslong protests across the country, known as the *Strajk Kobiet* (Women's Strike), which Szymanska-Medina also covered at the time. But the party's creeping control of the courts and the media was even more insidious. This is where Szymanska-Medina, who is known for addressing sociopolitical issues in her native Poland and elsewhere, aims to sound an alarm. Citing a warning by the political scientists Steven Levitsky and Daniel Ziblatt in their 2018 book *How Democracies Die*, she states that

"democracies die quietly 'with the slow, steady weakening of critical institutions, such as the judiciary and the press, as well as the gradual erosion of the long-standing political norms.' There is no need for tanks to roll out into the streets."

The "Good" Change focuses on judiciary reform—a particularly opaque mechanism, with grave and far-reaching consequences, by which PiS has slowly chipped away at Polish democracy. Szymanska-Medina tells the story, specifically, of a process of systematic repression of judges who challenged PiS's takeover of the courts, along with its unconstitutional changes. Polish judges were in a unique position to grasp the extent of PiS's power grab, as the party's methods of undermining juridical independence remain obscure to the layperson. Szymanska-Medina—and the judges she portrays—are conscious that this tactic is too often recognized only in retrospect, once serious repercussions are felt. The approach is familiar: from former US President Donald Trump's packing courts and his successful nomination of three Supreme Court justices, enabling the rollback of *Roe v. Wade* and threatening other civil liberties, to the complete overhaul of the courts in Belarus, cementing authoritarianism.

Szymanska-Medina engages photography at its most fundamental level, as the process of making something visible, then leveraging visibility as a countermechanism to the tactics of this right-wing government. She left Poland in 2004 to study in Berlin; in 2012, she pursued a program in photojournalism and documentary photography at the University of Applied Sciences and Arts in Hanover. Her practice has since been categorized by

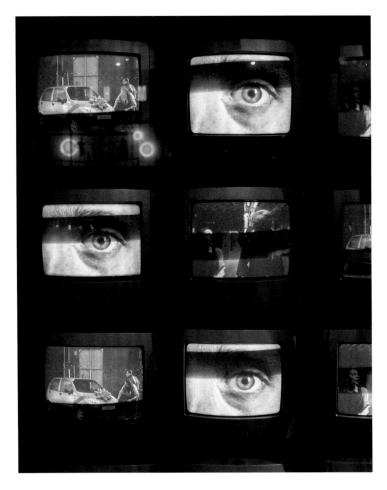

long-term projects broaching topics of sociopolitical significance, including recent work on underground abortion networks in Poland, human trafficking crossing Poland from Ukraine to Germany, the illegal disposal of German waste in Poland, and the experience of people living without running water or electricity deep in the Polish Carpathian mountains.

In the case of The "Good" Change—an appropriation of PiS's slogan, but exposing the menacing realities of the changes they've wrought—Szymanska-Medina published a free newspaper, printed with her own funds and the support of a few nonprofits dedicated to the defense of democracy, to be distributed in villages throughout Poland in the lead-up to the pivotal election last fall. (The quotation marks in the title are Szymanska-Medina's addition to the slogan, signaling her ironic use of the phrase.) She contextualizes the photographs with her own writing, as well as an essay by the Polish lawyer and human-rights activist Adam Bodnar.

Szymanska-Medina also incorporates partially redacted WhatsApp chat logs, positioning them in tandem with her photographs as images in their own right. The redacted lines—mostly names Szymanska-Medina blacked out to mitigate the risk of defamation accusations other journalists have been faced with—formally echo her interest in what is allowed to be seen. The irony here is that these screenshots are evidence of a smear campaign organized from inside the Ministry of Justice, with the express purpose of slandering and defaming judges who spoke out or acted against PiS. Szymanska-Medina originally received these transcripts from a confidential source but waited until the Polish news site Onet.pl broke the story, in 2019, to work publicly with them. The transcripts reveal PiS's strategy of leaking private information and stirring up fake news about judges, including accusations of infidelity and misappropriation of funds, which was then fomented by a troll Twitter account and fed to state-run media outlets.

In her portraits, Szymanska-Medina restores a sense of dignity and humanity to the judges targeted in these humiliation campaigns. She emphasizes that they are the ones who stood on the right side of history. The photographs are classical—each judge poses in the pews of the courtroom, many wearing or holding part of their official dress. In their faces, in the subtlety of their expressions, a palpable resolve, an ambivalent determination, rises to the fore.

Szymanska-Medina's newsprint publication lays out these stories for Polish voters, tracing the course of events from WhatsApp to collages of partially redacted tweets to images of smear campaigns being carried out on state TV. The publication serves to prompt voters: Now that you know, where will you stand? With a record voter turnout of 73 percent in the 2023 election, it was clear in retrospect that, like Szymanska-Medina, many Poles were moved to take a stance against the reign of right-wing corruption. Her work remains an urgent reminder to prevent the degradation of Polish democracy from happening again.

Szymanska-Medina's project conveys a belief in the power of human faces, and of information presented clearly and soberly, to strike a chord that the sensationalism of propaganda and fake news can't hit. Szymanska-Medina, in her confidence that telling the story straight, with empathy, is enough, extends the same respect to her viewers and her readers. While the election results were a relief for many Polish citizens, and for Szymanska-Medina too, her visual activism remains essential for the lived experience of this recent history to be remembered and not repeated.

Camila McHugh is a writer and curator
based in Berlin.

This page:
Army officers at Piłsudski
Square, Warsaw, April 10,
2021; opposite: The
suspended judge Piotr
Gąciarek on television
during a debate at the
Polsat TV station, Warsaw,
October 18, 2021

Abdo Shanan

The Right to a Memory

Tausif Noor

In a pivotal scene in Gillo Pontecorvo's 1966 film *The Battle of Algiers*, which tracks the strategic operations of the National Liberation Front during the early years of Algeria's war of independence against France, three female militants clandestinely deposit bombs in a crowded area patronized by French citizens. The camera briefly pauses on a boy licking an ice cream cone; within a few seconds, the bombs detonate. History erupts: revolutionaries become martyrs, and the pangs of Algeria's birth as a nation begin.

Financed by the Algerian government after independence was achieved in 1962, Pontecorvo's critically acclaimed film played a crucial role in circulating the names and images of Algerian revolutionaries such as Ali La Pointe, Hassiba Ben Bouali, and Djamila Bouhired (who played herself), cementing the Algerian War as a model of triumphant, hard-won anticolonial revolution. But what of the nation and its people *after* revolution, now half a century later? Who would document their faces and tell their stories, these people who lived too long to be venerated as martyrs, who were and remain distant from the halls of political power and celebrity?

In *The Right to a Memory* (2023), Abdo Shanan set out to build an archive of Algeria's ordinary citizens, combining crowdsourced vernacular pictures with his own recent portraits and street photography. Shanan—who was born in the Algerian city of Oran to a Sudanese father and an Algerian mother, and spent much of his life in Libya before returning to Algeria in his late twenties—had previously recorded the travails of his countrymen in *Diary: Exile* (2014–16), a series of photographs taken at jaunty, irregular angles to mirror the fractured state of the nation. His most recent project emerged, he tells me, from his frustration with the perception of Algeria as a country

Abdo Shanan, Two women,
Algiers, 2023

of martyrs. "To me, it's like we don't exist as living people," he says. "We talk only about the dead, and most of the pictures are of these heroes of the war of independence, even if they're still alive."

Many of the political revolutionaries who survived the tumult of the 1950s and '60s became major players in the fledgling Algerian national government—a fact that only hastened their transformation into icons, as illustrated by one of Shanan's images, which shows an array of postcards that are peddled streetside in Algiers. At the center is a three-ring binder, splayed open to reveal postcards in protective sheets: portraits of heads of state in postindependence Algeria, major military figures, and martyrs who fought for, but never lived to see, an independent nation. The seriality and reproducibility of these figures' likenesses reinforces the historian Benedict Anderson's argument that a nation is an imagined community held together by the bonds of shared language, standardized time, and the circulation of newspapers and media through print capitalism.

For all their charisma and the promise of their platforms, when lifted to the status of secular icons Algeria's political figures remain frozen in time, stultified and unable to speak to the pressures of the present moment. In this light, Shanan's photograph of the entrance to the Maqam Echahid, or Martyrs' Memorial, is a document of the state's capacity to honor the sacrifices of its citizens, but also to regulate and normalize national memory. Opened to the public on the twentieth anniversary of independence, in 1982, the Maqam is a sweeping concrete edifice, comprising three abstracted palm leaves (symbolizing national industry, land, and culture), dedicated to the unnamed martyrs of the independence war. When Shanan went to visit the monument for this project, a laconic security guard ushered him to the ticket counter but forbade him from taking photographs. "I felt I was entering a state-owned private collection of our own history," he says.

Shanan's experience lays bare the distance between the *nation* as a people with shared histories and cultural practices, and the *nation-state* as the entity that attempts at every turn to force these practices into predetermined forms, often without regard for the life within its bounds: maps penned with arbitrary borders, museums stale with sanctioned narratives. To counter such narratives, Shanan turned to multiplicity. After putting out a call on social media for Algerians to offer up their personal family photographs, which he would digitize in exchange for their use in his project, Shanan culled hundreds of images from dozens of contributors to form a populist, quotidian array of life in Algeria, from the years immediately following independence to the early 2000s.

In contrast to the staid monochrome images of familiar martyrs, the pictures Shanan received display small moments of celebration and joy: a group of men in tuxes and shirtsleeves gathered around a long table, heavy with dishes; a trio of revelers in a plush living room, smiling gleefully at the camera. Studio portraits and casual snapshots alike reflect the nation's half century of transformation, from hairstyles to advancements in camera and color technology, but they also evidence forms of continuity: traditional attire and jewelry that are still worn today. The images collectively capture the conviviality between flesh-and-blood people that persists across all those decades, the very pulse of what it means to be a nation.

This page:
Photo album, 1980s–'90s;
opposite: Abdo Shanan,
Camera and books, Algiers,
2023

Tausif Noor is a curator and critic whose work has appeared in the *New York Review of Books*, the *New Yorker*, and the *New York Times*.

This page:
School pictures, 1990s;
opposite: Abdo Shanan,
Mural of Mohamed
Belouizdad, an Algerian
militant and chief of
Special Organization,
the military branch of the
Algerian People's Party,
Algiers, 2023

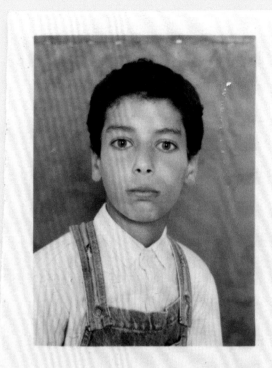

This page:
Images from an unknown
family album, 1980s;
opposite: Abdo Shanan,
Martyrs' Memorial, Algiers,
2023

All photographs from
the series *The Right to
a Memory*, 2023
Courtesy the artist

Naomieh Jovin
Descendants

Edwidge Danticat

Recently, moving to New York from Miami, after living there for over two decades, with each box I packed I wrestled with what to let go and what to keep. There was no hesitation about the family photo-albums, many of which I'd inherited from my mother after she died eight years ago. Each plastic-sheathed photograph is unique, some taken in photography studios in Port-au-Prince, others with my father's oversize camera in 1970s New York, and some Polaroids that had long faded, leaving behind only silhouettes. Those albums were a large part of my family's history—baptisms, christenings, weddings, funerals, visits to Haiti, church celebrations, rare vacations—until cell phones came along.

That young people are now returning to film cameras and digital point-and-shoots, blending a world of old and new, makes work by the photographer Naomieh Jovin both of its time and timeless. Merging family archives with close-up and detailed photographs of body parts, Jovin employs the type of fragmentation and lacunae that the telling of intergenerational immigrant stories sometimes demands. She calls on present and past, clothed and unclothed, young and old, well and unwell, secular and religious bodies to create an arresting interconnected call-and-response visual narrative.

Migration is rarely an individual affair. Jovin was born in Philadelphia to parents who immigrated to the United States from Haiti in the early 1980s. "Since middle school, I used to bring my baby album with me and sit at lunch flipping through the pages," Jovin has said. "I loved looking at the amazing outfits my parents put me in for my birthdays. Dressed like a true Haitian baby! I also enjoyed looking back at old photographs and trying to figure out the story behind them."

For first- or second-generation immigrants, the stories behind the photographs in our family albums are sometimes purposefully hidden from us, because they are too painful to tell. The people whose faces we are looking at might have been wounded in some way, either before or after these photographs were taken. As demonstrated by the cutouts in some of Jovin's images, absence is as tangible as presence. The archival materials in the pictures, including the diplomas, the unopened bills, the ceramic animals and fruit, illustrate gaps that Jovin attempts to fill, at times, with incorporeal and disembodied hands, seemingly reaching out to take hold of these stories.

Images like the ones in Jovin's family albums are archived in many Haitian and Haitian-diaspora households, sometimes

Page 106:
Is Manmi in heaven, 2022;
this page: *Untitled*, 2022;
opposite: *Madame Lucien*,
2021; following spread
and 112: *Untitled*, 2021;
page 113: *Untitled*
(Daddy's Toolbox), 2020

All photographs from
the series *Gwo Fanm*,
2017–ongoing
Courtesy the artist

with notes scribbled on the back, often from lovers pleading from a distance not to be forgotten. With the photograph titled *Madame Lucien* (2021), of a young woman standing in front of a Japanese-garden backdrop, we expect that kind of sentiment. But Jovin tells us that the superimposed words are part of a breakup note from Madame Lucien: "Life is a flower and a blow. Very often, right next to joy, pleasure, and laughter, there are always tears and sorrow that bring ugliness and darkness to our existence. Because Life is made of separation, I must bend to the laws of nature."

Often, when an older Haitian person dies, the picture chosen for the cover of their funeral program is of them in their prime, when they were at their most handsome or beautiful. We look at these faces from the present and the past and can't help but wonder what our descendants might look like, who they will resemble, where they might live. How much of all this incidental archive might they let go of, and what might they keep? Will it be the indoor or outdoor pictures? Those portraits in the barbershop or living room? Or those out in nature, with flowing streams and rocks? Will it be the communion one or the nudes? Or will it be the *fanfa*, the funeral band accompanying the mourners and their massive bouquet of flowers to the cemetery?

In November 2020, a photo-essay by Jovin in *The Nation* made its way to me via friends and family WhatsApp groups. "There Is a Name for Women Like My Mother" read the headline. The piece was mainly about Jovin's mother, but most Haitians know someone who's been called *gwo fanm*—"big woman"— in either a complimentary or derogatory way. Jovin's mother was in the favorable category. A smart dresser and hard worker who'd sponsored many family members to come to the United States, she died of breast cancer when Jovin was ten, making it understandable that Jovin would spend so much time looking at her baby album as a girl. These images were her way of communing with her mother and *tout sa n pa wè yo*, a Creole expression meaning "all those who are no longer visible, those who can no longer see." That photo-album made Jovin's mother visible to her.

"Even in death, she took up space," Jovin writes.

She calls her project *Gwo Fanm* (2017–ongoing), describing a *gwo fanm* as "a woman who stands out in life and stands up for the ones they love. But a Gwo Fanm is also a woman who takes more than their fair share of the slings and arrows this world throws at them, absorbs hurt and pain that could crush less resilient or determined people."

Jovin, too, is a *gwo fanm*, as an aunt once told her, based partly on her success as a photographer.

"So much of the immigrant experience is one of loss, loss of the community they leave behind, loss of the history in their home country," Jovin writes. "By creating these photos of the women in my family, and reclaiming the images they made during their lifetimes, I hope to forestall this loss, to show the purpose and honor that defined their lives, and to actively create a new narrative for my generation."

Edwidge Danticat's most recent book
is *Everything Inside: Stories* (2019).
She teaches at Columbia University.

Alice Proujansky

Fighting Times

A photographer reconstructs her parents' radical past, and reckons with what to keep and what to let go.
Piper French

fg. 19 - The Question That You Ask - script

item 45 Ellen Moves Camp   :20
    I think that we'll make it in the long run, even if we don't our
children will. You know they call us militant and they call us savages,
but I think they're gonna have some real militants when our children
grow up, uou know. And our grand children grow up, uou know. They see
this and they know what's happening.

item 46 music   :49   6 slides at 5 secs each, Resting til
                            End on last slide,

Page 114:
Jed Proujansky stands
for a mug shot following
his arrest during
Weatherman's Days of
Rage in Chicago, 1969;
previous page: Materials
from a slideshow Jed
Proujansky and Joan Deely
used in their organizing,
2022

This page:
Alice Proujansky at about
nine years old, ca. 1989

Amid the radical imagery of Alice Proujansky's project *Hard Times are Fighting Times* (2023), the presence of something as conventional as a baby book stops you in your tracks. One of many objects the photographer has held on to from her childhood, the book contains a delicate illustration of a woman clutching her swaddled infant and the words "Mother and Father's Ambitions for Baby." The whole thing arrests for seeming so bourgeois. But squint and you'll see that Proujansky's father has scrawled, in the space left blank for these intentions: *To grow up and be anything that you want, except a fascist or a banker.*

What could have led Proujansky's parents to articulate such a wish for their child? *Hard Times are Fighting Times*, a visual record of their unconventional lives as leftist radicals, provides an answer. The project is a catalog of the couple's involvement in the New Left and its factions during the 1960s and '70s as they moved between Chicago, Vermont, Philadelphia, and Minneapolis. Proujansky's father, Jed, was a member of Weatherman, the far-left organization that splintered off from Students for a Democratic Society (SDS); her mother, Joan Deely, joined the Prairie Fire Organizing Committee, an above-ground arm of the group established after Weatherman leaders went into hiding as the Weather Underground; both later belonged to the Native American Solidarity Committee. It was a time of flux and crisis for the American left, as disagreements about tactics produced fissures, activists sought new causes after the end of the Vietnam War, and the government cracked down on young revolutionaries with renewed force. In a police snapshot taken after his arrest

PRISONS: WHO GOES AND WHY?

5

Spread from *Attica: Then and Now, Still Fighting Back* (1978)

during Weatherman's Days of Rage protests in Chicago, Alice's father looks alert, defiant, but also a little shell-shocked, as though he's wondering what the hell he's gotten himself into.

In 1970, a bomb the Weather Underground was fashioning in the basement of a Greenwich Village townhouse went off accidentally, destroying the building and killing three young members. Today the explosion tends to be invoked as a sort of shorthand for the failures and excesses of the New Left. Jed, as Proujansky told me when we spoke last fall, "was in Cuba with the Venceremos brigade when the townhouse bombing happened and came home and was like, Where is everybody?" Joan, meanwhile, became disillusioned by everything from Prairie Fire's ritualistic criticism of members to yet another splinter group's infamous 1981 Brink's heist, which left three dead and several young radicals in prison for life, or close to it. "I was out," Joan told me. "I ended up working at a battered women's shelter. To me, that was a form of activism that made sense."

But both Jed and Joan's reasons for getting involved with the New Left, from his admiration for the early civil rights movement to her horror at the Vietnam War and desire to live differently from generations of women before her, also reveal the liberatory promises of such work. "My goal has always been to change the US government as we know it," Jed told me. For Proujansky, the idea of making a project about her parents' movement years had percolated for some time, but it was Donald Trump's election in 2016 that cemented her decision—not because

The project is a catalog of the couple's involvement in the New Left and its factions during the 1960s and '70s.

she experienced the event as an absolute breach with the past, but because she wanted people to understand that we'd been here before.

Throughout *Hard Times*, Proujansky interweaves contemporary photographs she has taken of her family, in black and white, with images and ephemera that illustrate her parents' past lives, including her father's FBI dossier, which he retrieved in 1979 thanks to a Freedom of Information Act request. These once-secret files include pages of redacted observations on his movements, a transcript of monosyllabic phone calls with the Weather Underground leader Bill Ayers, and even an uncharitable physical description ("5′9″ and 135 pounds, slender and unemployed," his daughter recites to me, snorting at the kicker).

Proujansky likes to call her project "a people's history and a person's history." It is simultaneously grand and intimate in scale, encompassing the liberation struggles of families everywhere—from Harlem, to the White Earth Reservation in Minneapolis, to Vietnam—and the portrait of one family over a lifetime. Images like that of the baby book hint at the weight of two different types of inheritance: the universal and the particular. "Not everybody's parents have FBI files," she remarked when we spoke. "Most of us have to negotiate parental expectation—how much of this do we want to carry forward? How much do we want to leave behind?"

Growing up in rural western Massachusetts, Proujansky didn't know much about her parents' past lives. She could tell they had strong views: her mom refused to buy her Barbies, and her dad hosted "US out of Central America" meetings accompanied by a distinct odor that she later identified as marijuana. A sticker on the fridge read "I'd rather be smashing imperialism." Didn't

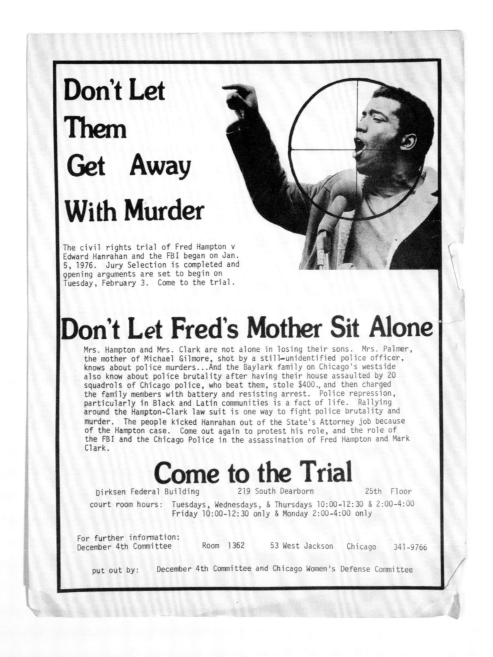

Don't Let Them Get Away With Murder

The civil rights trial of Fred Hampton v Edward Hanrahan and the FBI began on Jan. 5, 1976. Jury Selection is completed and opening arguments are set to begin on Tuesday, February 3. Come to the trial.

Don't Let Fred's Mother Sit Alone

Mrs. Hampton and Mrs. Clark are not alone in losing their sons. Mrs. Palmer, the mother of Michael Gilmore, shot by a still-unidentified police officer, knows about police murders...And the Baylark family on Chicago's westside also know about police brutality after having their house assaulted by 20 squadrols of Chicago police, who beat them, stole $400., and then charged the family members with battery and resisting arrest. Police repression, particularly in Black and Latin communities is a fact of life. Rallying around the Hampton-Clark law suit is one way to fight police brutality and murder. The people kicked Hanrahan out of the State's Attorney job because of the Hampton case. Come out again to protest his role, and the role of the FBI and the Chicago Police in the assassination of Fred Hampton and Mark Clark.

Come to the Trial

Dirksen Federal Building   219 South Dearborn   25th Floor

court room hours: Tuesdays, Wednesdays, & Thursdays 10:00-12:30 & 2:00-4:00
Friday 10:00-12:30 only & Monday 2:00-4:00 only

For further information:
December 4th Committee   Room 1362   53 West Jackson   Chicago   341-9766

put out by: December 4th Committee and Chicago Women's Defense Committee

everyone's parents get together around Thanksgiving with a coterie of comrades that included a Black Panther exonerated from death row, a capital defense lawyer, and hospice nurses who worked with early AIDS patients?

Prep school and a move to New York to attend NYU, where she studied photography, would disabuse her of that impression. After graduation, Proujansky stayed in the city and began teaching, mostly in public schools. In her photographic series focusing on abortion care and alternative birth practices, Native coming-of-age ceremonies, and a lesbian poet who belonged to the Jewish Labor Bund, she depicts the deep sense of solidarity undergirding care work and alternative ways of living. "Doing photo-essays has always been the best medium for me because the images need to be able to talk to each other," Proujansky told me. "It's not about finding just one great picture that supposedly tells the whole story—there's a narrative." But to some extent, her decision to pursue documentary photography was also bound up in her parents' notion of what constituted a worthwhile life—"an answer to the question that's *always* been in my mind about, like, Am I doing enough? Am I radical, am I changing enough?" she said. It seems likely that there are, in fact,

a few choices beyond "fascist" and "banker" that they may not have approved of.

Proujansky's thematic focus on maternal health seems almost preordained: her parents gave her a camera to document her younger sister's birth. "I started when I was seven," she said. But there are few family snapshots from her early years. For Proujansky's parents, those heady decades spent fighting for radical social change were accompanied by the sensation of being constantly watched. This was the height of COINTELPRO, the illegal FBI counterintelligence program that monitored and undermined activist organizations, and there were informants everywhere. Jed would hear clicks on the line during phone calls, a sign he was being wiretapped. Photography was associated with state surveillance—anyone who brought a camera along to a demonstration was not to be trusted. "Most pictures taken were done by the police," he noted.

Some fifty years on, Proujansky has assumed the role of detective and turned her camera on her parents. Rarely is any life—its dramas and banalities and lost moments—afforded so much scrutiny; there is an irony in the fact that Jed and Joan's most dedicated archivists have been the FBI and their own

Brothers

International Women's Day is a celebration to honor the history and tradition of women's struggles. It is a holiday of the people, celebrated in this country as well as the countries of Cuba, China, and Vietnam. It is important to us, as men, to recognize the role of women in the struggles for liberation against imperialism. The feminist movement has a positive effect on the lives of men throughout the world. It helps us to fight against our sexism and make positive steps in our personal and collective relationships, in our work and in our play.

Let us join in the celebration

Come join

Saturday, March 8, at N.S.P. Plaza
(5th and Nicollet)

march and Rally

at 2:: PM at the YMCA, 30 S. 9th St. Mpls.

to demand;
— a ceiling on food industry profits and a nutritionally adequate food stamp program.
— effective, safe birth control and abortion and an end to population control programs administered by the U.S. government at home and abroad.
— End of aid to thieu and Lon Nol, implement the peace agreement.
— Freedom for Wounded Knee defendents.
— an end to discriminatory lay-offs of women.
— We support and affirm the freedom of sexual preference and demand an end to discrimination against homosexuals.

A poster for International Women's Day, with text written by Jed, Minneapolis, 1975

There is an irony in the fact that Jed and Joan's most dedicated archivists have been the FBI and their own daughter.

daughter. She plays with these parallels, teasing out the connections between the penetrating gaze of the state and the watchful eye of a child, and also showing the qualitative difference in the sorts of images they produce.

Proujansky, who is also a teacher, started out showing photographs to her high school art students and asking them what the images sparked in their minds (tellingly, some kids saw her father's mug shot and assumed it depicted a criminal that her dad, presumably a cop, was chasing). She recently published a book of the work, which has allowed her to present images in two categories—"the family" and "the archive"—that start out distinct, only to dissolve as the pages progress. A "family" shot of Proujansky's young daughter depicts her nestled on a sofa opening a birthday present, surrounded by relatives. Her blond hair is illuminated by a sunbeam passing through the window. Another shows Proujansky's son playfully wrestling with his cousin in the yard.

These are scenes of total innocence and tranquility—or they would be if this were a different project. Here, they're interrupted by materials Proujansky has drawn from her parents' records, including a flyer urging onlookers to attend the trial in the civil rights case of Fred Hampton, the murdered Black Panther leader. "Don't let them get away with murder," it implores, accompanied by an image of Hampton with a target superimposed over his head.

"Did Fred Hampton's grandchildren get to do this?" Proujansky asked, gesturing at the family photos. "No, they didn't." Hampton never even met his own child—his fiancée was almost

Jed and his friends in the
yard of their commune,
Bread and Roses,
Minneapolis, 1975.
Photograph by Gayla Ellis

nine months pregnant when law enforcement agents burst into
their Chicago apartment and shot him dead.

For the Black Liberation Army, an offshoot of the Black
Panthers, white radicals were useful precisely because they were
"invisible" to law enforcement—they blended in. This also meant
that they could step away from the heat of the struggle with fewer
lasting consequences. "There is a real unfairness," Proujansky
said, in the fact that her family could have both: the revolutionary
commitments and the domestic idyll.

But it also required a sacrifice of another order. "That was
all I did," Joan told me, thinking back on her movement years.
"I just put a lot of my life on hold while I was doing this very intense
work. I couldn't do that when I had small children. It was apparent
to me that there's only so much of a person to go around." Jed
eventually took an unfulfilling database job. Bills needed to be
paid. Still, Proujansky refuses cynicism or defeatism about where
the "don't trust anybody over thirty" generation has ended up,
choosing instead to highlight the ways her parents have carried
forth their ideals, including by passing them on to their children.

During our conversation, Proujansky pointed me toward
a photograph of a yellow poster with a stylized rose at its center,
created by her father for International Women's Day in 1975.
In it, Jed writes of "an end to discrimination against homosexuals";
today, we might see a call for trans rights instead. He urges a
peace agreement and an end to aid to despotic rulers in Vietnam
and Cambodia; over the weeks Proujansky, her parents, and I
communicated, Americans across the country demanded a ceasefire

and cessation of US military aid to Israel as the country rained bombs on Gaza. "You look at that poster, and it mentions a lot of things that people are specifically fighting for now, it's just in different language," Proujansky said. To her, the poster could either invite despair at how little has changed—or spur the recognition that resistance to injustice is an intergenerational battle. "It's called a struggle for a reason," she added.

Proujansky is a restless, energetic conversationalist, quick to interrupt herself or interrogate a point she's just made. She is relentlessly interested in the *why* of it: what it was about Jed and Joan that made them leave relatively comfortable middle-class lives and go out to do the things they did. She also insists on foregrounding her own point of view—the extent to which everything we're seeing is filtered through her perspective. "I always say that photographs aren't windows," she told me. "They're authored." Between the authoritative language of the state and the emphatic nature of the activists' posters and flyers, she is striving for something more ambivalent and conflicted, something that attempts to probe at her parents' psychological formation and inevitably displays her own, too. The goal is not to create a false equivalence between a repressive government and the people who fight back against it; she is clear about where her loyalties lie. But it feels like an answer to her question about any child's lifelong negotiation: what to keep, what to let go.

**Piper French is a writer based in
Los Angeles.**

OUTLAWS of AMERIKA

communiques
from the
weather
underground

New from Aperture

aperture

**I'm So Happy You Are Here:
Japanese Women Photographers
from the 1950s to Now**
US $75.00 / UK £60.00

**Zanele Muholi:
Somnyama Ngonyama
Hail the Dark Lioness, Vol. II**
US $85.00 / UK £70.00

**Kelli Connell:
Pictures for Charis**
US $65.00 / UK £50.00

**Myriam Boulos:
What's Ours**
US $55.00 / UK £42.95

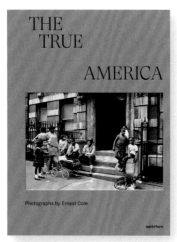

**Ernest Cole:
The True America**
US $65.00 / UK £50.00

**Pao Houa Her:
My grandfather turned into a tiger
. . . and other illusions**
US $60.00 / UK £50.00

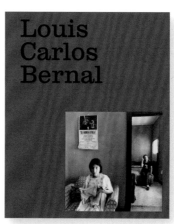

**Louis Carlos Bernal:
Monografía**
US $50.00 / UK £40.00

**Zhang Xiao:
Community Fire**
US $65.00 / UK £50.00

Shop: aperture.org/books

The PhotoBook Review

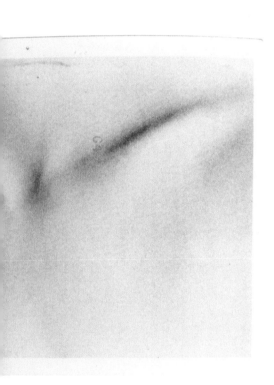

Jean Pierre DELAGE
12 rue Custine
PARIS, FRANCE
75018
AIR MAIL

⑦

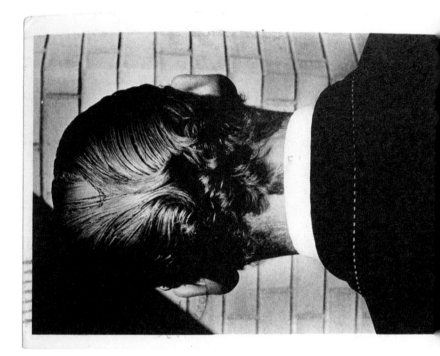

THE ILLUMINATED MAN, 1969
PHOTOGRAPH BY DUANE MICHALS

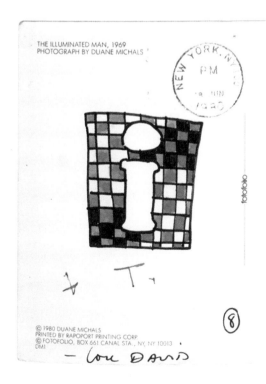

© 1980 DUANE MICHALS
PRINTED BY RAPOPORT PRINTING CORP
© FOTOFOLIO, BOX 661 CANAL STA., NY, NY 10013 •
DM1
— Lou DAVIS

Jean Pierre DELA
12 rue Custine
PARIS, FRANC
75018
AIR MAIL

⑧

The Artist's Library

Rebecca Bengal in Conversation with Ari Marcopoulos

Ari Marcopoulos's personal library reflects kinetic engagements with subcultures of the world that connect to his own wide-ranging work. "Already, look, we're surrounded by them," Marcopoulos, a photographer and filmmaker, said during a recent visit at his Brooklyn home, where a capacious, free-flowing arrangement of books lines the walls of an upstairs landing. More than eighty boxes were packed into his studio for an upcoming move. Marcopoulos has published some two hundred books and zines of his own (*Zines*, a collection of the latter, was published in 2023 by Aperture). He is refreshingly unconcerned about the preciousness of the books and magazines

he collects. With equal admiration, he cited a rare, expensive edition of Yutaka Takanashi's *Toshi-e* (*Towards the City*, 1974) bought in Japan; a notebook by the filmmaker Pedro Costa, fascinating though "honestly, badly printed and shittily made," he tells me; and a vintage *Life* that his partner, Kara Walker, gave him—the dynamic design of its cover, he explained, featuring Wilt Chamberlain and Kareem Abdul-Jabbar, struck him when he first saw it in 1972. From his collection Marcopoulos culled a few stacks, which he spread out on a long kitchen table—a microcosm of both the photobooks that triggered a life in art and the ones he turns to now.

Rebecca Bengal: **Tell me about the first photobook that made an impression on you.**

Ari Marcopoulos: I grew up in a town called Haren, quite close to Amsterdam, and back then, even on television, you were able to see Fassbinder or Pasolini movies. I remember seeing early Godard movies on TV and being very confused about what it was all about. But I also knew that that's what I should go after. I became interested in visual arts. The first photobook I got was this exhibition catalog of Maria Austria, and it's inscribed: "Given to me by my father after visit to Stedelijk Museum." I was probably sixteen, seventeen, around 1977, because that's when I think I started taking pictures and making Super 8 films.

RB: What was it about Maria Austria's work that engaged you at that age?

AM: Her photographs were fascinating to me. Portraits of Samuel Beckett, James Baldwin, Bertrand Russell, Albert Schweitzer, Igor Stravinsky, and then also black-and-white photographs, mostly of performances, done in low light, so there's a certain amount of blurriness to them. She's documenting something—Happenings in Holland, all in the late 1960s and early 1970s.

RB: For you, were they a gateway into the worlds she was documenting?

AM: I think from that exposure, I started going more to Amsterdam, seeing shows by James Turrell and Robert Rauschenberg. Then my dad, who was a commercial airline pilot, brought back a camera from Japan. That was something that really fascinated me, the camera. Just the instrument. Just looking through it, figuring it out without even taking pictures, thinking about how it would work.

RB: What's one of the first books you bought on your own?

AM: *Diane Arbus* (1972), which was published by Aperture. Another was *Portraits*, by Richard Avedon (1976). When I moved to the United States, in 1980, I became way more aware of what was happening in photography. I bought the book *Walker Evans: American Photographs* (1975), which was a show at the Museum of Modern Art. And then, *The Americans* (1998), although that's not my favorite Robert Frank book.

RB: What's your favorite?

AM: Probably *The Lines of My Hand* (1972). It's sort of a history of his photography that ends with the Nova Scotia stuff. I also love *Pangnirtung* (2011), one of Robert's later books. He goes to the Northwest Territories. It's farther north than Nova Scotia [where Frank had a house with his wife, June Leaf]. He goes there with a friend, and he takes these photographs that are all done with a Polaroid negative. They're somber landscapes in the beginning. In the first picture, you see a boat, that's the human presence, then more landscapes. Then you see this sort of built wall with a chain-link fence at the airport, followed by a telephone post. And then, as you go along, he shows all the windows of these Inuit homes. It's a very simple, very beautiful book.

RB: You and Frank were friends?

Opposite:
The artist's library
bookshelf, New York, 2023

This page and page 128:
Selections from the artist's collection, including photobooks by Hitomi Watanabe, Tatsuo Kurihara, Osamu Nagahama and Mineo Higashi, Riho Mishimoto, Kikujiro Fukushima, Tadao Mitome, Walker Evans, Diane Arbus, Richard Avedon, and Larry Clark
Photographs by Ari Marcopoulos for *Aperture*

Photobooks and novels are equal in my admiration, but I don't think they're equal in what they do for me.

AM: Yes. I asked him about that book two or three months before he died [in 2019]. He just told me how he got there—by plane. And here's this book by Robert called *good days quiet* (2019), the last book that he did. These are mostly pictures from Nova Scotia in the winter.

RB: What draws you to his later publications?

AM: *The Americans* is a brilliant book, but that's all people talked about when it came to Robert's work. And I was much more interested in his interior, which, I feel, comes out way more in the later books where you really get to see this raw interior of Robert's thoughts.

RB: You seem to have every edition of *The Lines of My Hand*. Are there any sorts of photobooks that you consciously collect?

AM: I collect books about Japanese protest movements in the 1960s, which happened around many things, including the extension of Narita Airport, where they were taking farmland away and the farmers were fighting the police. And the Japanese Communist Party and a lot of students joined the farmers. I came upon those books by chance, because I am very much into photographers like Moriyama, Araki, and others. I was already looking at their work, but then Phil Aarons—he is one of the big supporters of Printed Matter—showed me all of the early Xerox books that Araki did. They're just handmade books.

RB: Which is something you do too.

AM: Yes. The idea of the Provoke movement—and the word already says it—was that they wanted to destroy photography as it was. They didn't want to have pretty pictures or colorful pictures or even narrative pictures. They just wanted to have images. So, you get a lot of high-contrast, black-and-white, grainy photographs. And that really fascinated me. They helped me let go of my fear of technical proficiency. I think mistakes are the best possibility, the best impetus to go forward in what you're trying to do.

RB: **There's something compelling about that lack of clarity and the ambiguity.**

AM: I don't speak Japanese or read Japanese, but the photographs give me some information. There were also protests in Okinawa. For instance, here is an amazing book [of pictures made in Okinawa by another Provoke photographer], *The Island of Long Hot Nights* (1972), photographed by Osamu Nagahama. It's all horizontal photographs. There are these blue pages that look almost like Risograph prints. I got it at Alias Books in LA, a great store, and the book dealer there later said, "Oh, I should have never sold it to you."

I also have this book called *Forest of Pressure* (2006). It's not a photobook, but it

illustrates my obsession. It's about Ogawa Pro, a Japanese film collective that started filming these protests, and then making movies about farming, and then going around with a 16mm projector and showing them in little community centers in small farming towns—to start a revolution, to make people aware.

RB: **And with this next one you have here, which is LaToya Ruby Frazier's *The Notion of Family* (Aperture, 2014), you could almost say that you see the interiority you admire in Frank, with him photographing close to his home, mixed with the long-fought protests by Japanese farming communities.**

AM: I love *The Notion of Family*. This is another document of what American imperialism, segregation, and economic war on the people does to a community, to a family. It's about Frazier's dedication, her tenacity, to really dig in deep and stick with it.

RB: **Do you find you tend to favor a certain size or scope of a photobook, whether it's one you're making or one you are looking at?**

AM: I more look at it from the perspective of what you're trying to express in a book.

I mean, I made a book that has twelve hundred pages—it's like a telephone book. But I'm also very into books that are smaller in size, that you could put in a backpack. Larry Clark's *Tulsa* (1971) is very tightly edited. I think it has around seventy-two photographs. The book has power because of that. But then, with Moriyama's *Hokkaido* (2008), with close to two thousand images, the power is in the almost impossibility of really looking at that book in one session. There's no formula.

RB: **The writer Hua Hsu has talked about how writing to different lengths, from essays to his memoir, *Stay True* (2022), reflects making mixtape cassettes—60 minutes, 90 minutes, 120 minutes.**

AM: Often when I get approached by publishers to do a book, I'll ask, "How big do you think we should make it?" And they look at me very strangely. I'll say, maybe, "Well, let's make it 8.5 by 11, letter size. And shall we do 100 pages or 120 pages?" And then, they look at me very strangely again, like, What? Because I kind of design the container ahead of time, and from there, I adjust.

RB: **Can photobooks be their own form of literature? How are they distinct from, say, a great novel?**

AM: Photography is a medium that lends itself very well to books. More so than a lot of other mediums. Photobooks and novels are equal in my admiration, but I don't think they're equal in what they do for me. They're suited for different things. And I was just talking about this with Takashi Homma, that literature has more of an ability to do away with cutting out the periphery. Photographs are slices out of things. And then, with all these slices, you make something. But do you really get a sense of smell and premonition, of insecurity or confidence, all at the same time? Not like in a novel. That's why there are novels and photobooks—they can coexist.

Rebecca Bengal is the author of *Strange Hours: Photography, Memory, and the Lives of Artists* (Aperture, 2023).

A Peculiar Feeling of Reality

Pati Hill turns xerography into a pliable and surprising form of photographic art.
Simon Wu

Pati Hill in her studio in Sens, France, with her work *The Copier Angels* (1997–98), late 1990s

"This stocky, unrevealing box stands 3 ft. high without stockings or feet and lights up like a Xmas tree no matter what I show it." So begins an entry about the photocopy machine, typed on a small placard, by Pati Hill, the American artist and writer, who was the subject of a small yet thrilling survey exhibition at New York's Printed Matter last fall. The entry continues: "[The photocopier] repeats my words perfectly as many times as I ask it to, but when I show it a hair curler it hands me back a spaceship, and when I show it the inside of a straw hat it describes the eerie joys of a descent into a volcano." To Hill's confusion and wonder, common objects become strange and beautiful. A hairbrush is the surface of a gloomy planet, teddy bears thrash in space, ribbons are bacterial colonies. In Hill's hands, xerography is a pliable—and underappreciated—form of photographic art.

Yet Hill did not arrive at xerography until the mid-1970s, after she had lived multiple lives—as a model (in *Harper's Bazaar*, no less), a writer (three novels, a memoir, a poetry collection, and short stories in the *Paris Review*), and a self-proclaimed housewife in France. The Printed Matter survey charted her life chronologically, assembling her varied creative outputs to render a portrait of someone who could be aptly described as an image/text engineer. Observing her life from its end, the viewer appreciates Hill as an artist in dogged pursuit of a language of her own—one that deployed word, sign, and image in equal measure.

The beginnings of that language appear in her earliest encounters with the camera: her modeling work. In one photograph, a young Hill looks away from the camera, in pigtails, clutching a copy of *Harper's Bazaar* from 1941. Another shows her in a polka-dot dress, with multiple outtakes presented in a makeshift grid. Perhaps the experience of modeling, of having her body molded in the light, informed her later work. There's something of that posturing in the deconstructed rose petals of *Untitled (petals)* (ca. 2000), as if the act of being an object compelled her to transform other objects. As she later wrote in her memoir, modeling gave her the "peculiar feeling of 'reality' . . . The reality of an object, maybe."

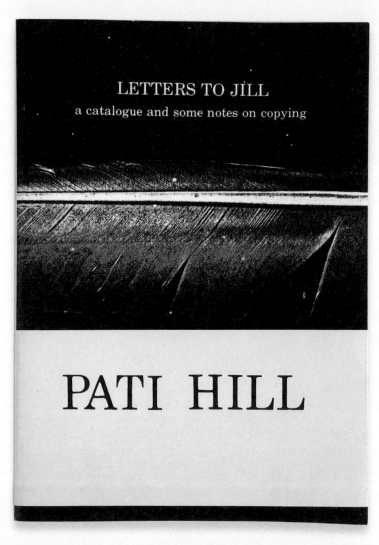

Cover of *Letters to Jill* (Self-published, 1979)

LETTERS TO JILL
a catalogue and some notes on copying

PATI HILL

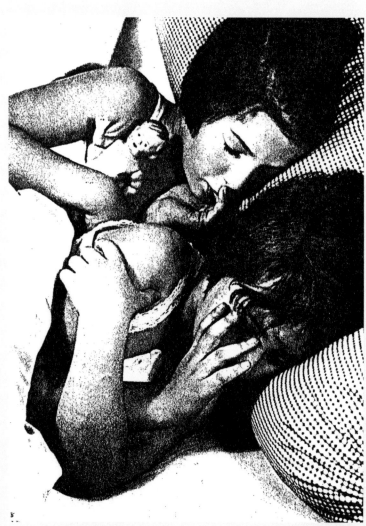

Xerograph from *Impossible Dreams* (Alice James Books, 1976)

In around 1973, Hill began to develop the language she would play with over the rest of her life. She had become a mother, and the mundanity of housework prompted her to start fiddling with the photocopier, a tool she later describes, in her 1979 book *Letters to Jill*, as a "found instrument, a saxophone without directions." Her 1975 book, *Slave Days*, features twenty-nine poems and thirty-one photocopier prints of small domestic objects—"choirs" of hairpins, an eraser as a metaphor for a life as a housewife, a cookie cutter as a celestial star. For *Dreams Objects Moments* (1976), she collected about a hundred "shallow, literal descriptions of dreams, objects, and moments," including of her dog Lucas, a weekend in the countryside, and dreams about being in the hold of a ship.

After a chance encounter with the designer Charles Eames, who was then working at IBM, on a flight from Paris to New York in 1977, Hill was set up with a state-of-the-art IBM Copier II in her home in Stonington, Connecticut. She began copying things like dead swans, children's clothing, and rose petals. That year, Hill published *Symbol Language*, which she wrote for her daughter, using text-and-image diagrams to experiment with symbolic language: a simple star means "want / wish / need / please / thank-you." Life is

**Pati Hill photographed
by Louise Dahl-Wolfe
for *Harper's Bazaar*,
August 1941**
All works courtesy the
Pati Hill Collection, Arcadia
University

Hill found traditional language so ridden with gender that she sought to escape it and produce her own.

a large "U" but death is an upside-down "U." Schematic drawings like "MALE AND FEMALE" offer detached, semiotic deconstructions of how gender operates in the written and lived world. This kind of deconstruction has the effect of turning the language back into a sign; a scratch of ink on the surface of a page. It seems Hill found traditional language so ridden with gender that she sought to escape it and produce her own.

Unlike a photograph, a xerograph— a copy—necessitates a bit of physical contact; one's subject must be amenable, or be made amenable, to a temporary sandwiching between sheets of glass. The contact alters the subject, attempts to press material that is three-dimensional into two dimensions. In the series *Untitled (ribbons)*, from about 1990, the slight lift from the

ribbons produces a scratchy, indeterminate ground. Sometimes the three-dimensional aspect is irreconcilable, as in *Untitled (dog)*, from around 1990; the dog's head recedes ominously into a kind of oblivion.

When applied to some materials, like the belongings of Hill's daughter, this technique gets more unnerving. Animals, teddy bears, plant matter, and bananas convey, when scanned, as in the 1975 *Slave Days* series, a curiously morbid quality, as if composing a memorial for childhood even as Hill's daughter was living it. You also wonder what the effect of being smushed under a copier had on her daughters' toys or pets. Sometimes Hill gets around this by taking "real life copies" (i.e., regular photographs): a small booklet labeled "Pati's cats" features images of her cats sitting on various glass surfaces, captured from different angles so that their bodies form organic blobs and curves. (I imagine she was never able to get her cats to sit still on a photocopier.) In this way, Hill's Xeroxes have a memento mori quality; one can imagine her subjects frozen in this state between decay and exuberance just long enough for the copier to capture them.

At the beginning of the Printed Matter exhibition, next to the modeling images from the 1940s, was Hill's *Self-portrait with a feather duster* (ca. 2000), a photomontage made nearly sixty years later. Here, Hill elongates her shadow using the sunlight coming through a doorway; you can just get a sense of her shape, wiggling in outline under the sun, cobbled together over the lines of various outtakes. These wobbly, shadowy collages are apt portraits of a shape-shifting polymath.

Harper's Bazaar, August 1941

The Pigtailers

LOUISE DAHL-WOLFE

• When we were very young, our nannies used to braid us tightly, rude little boys tweaked our plaits, and we were miserable and longed for flowing curls. But now, fully dressed and in our right minds, we have put our long bobs back into pigtails, bowing them at the ends, twisting them with ribbons and yarn, entwining them with flowers, and even wrapping them stiff with cotton tape, as the Indians do. We have turned the plain little-girl pigtail into something pretty, chic, and purely personal—as shown by the college girl above who wears hers with a fluffy pompadour bang and ties one tail with a blue ribbon, the other with a crimson.

49

Simon Wu is a New York–based writer and curator. His first book, *Dancing on My Own*, will be published in 2024.

Reviews

Hans Wilschut

Beirut Epi-Centre Ville

Cover of Hans Wilschut,
Beirut, Epi-Centre Ville
(Fw:Books, 2023)

Hans Wilschut

Among the most horrific reverberations of the Beirut port explosion of August 2020 was its sound. The detonation of 2,750 tons of ammonium nitrate produced a blast so powerful it was detected as a seismic event in Cyprus, more than 150 miles away across the Mediterranean Sea. Though most people viewed the destruction through camera-phone videos and followed dramatic tallies—over 220 dead, 7,000 injured, and 300,000 displaced—those in Beirut were reminded of familiar wounds

from a not-long-ago civil war, and of the recurring failures of Lebanon's political elite. "An explosion resonates across time," the author and translator Lina Mounzer wrote the morning after the blast. "The people of Beirut have been shaped by the bombs that reconfigured this country." The noise, in some form or other, persists.

Hans Wilschut's searching portraits of the aftermath are, in contrast, notably quiet. In *Beirut, Epi-Centre Ville* (Fw:Books, 2023; 128 pages, $34), the Dutch photographer attempts to register both the immediate and extended horror of the blast, choosing as his subjects the refigured urban facades of the city, often arranged in stark juxtapositions or stretched across full spreads. "I am looking for the signs of resistance in stillness," he writes in a brief essay. The book references an earlier project, *Beyrouth Centre Ville* (1992), for which six photographers traveled to the capital to photograph its devastated downtown after the end of the civil war in 1990. Among them were Josef Koudelka, Robert Frank, Fouad Elkoury, and Gabriele Basilico, the Italian photographer of cityscapes who helped shape Wilschut's relationship to the urban space.

Like its precedent, *Beirut, Epi-Centre Ville* features almost no photographs of people. "They are absent but omnipresent," writes the Lebanese novelist Dominique Eddé, who contributed an essay to both books, "behind the windows, the holes, the hundred-times remade fabric of their city." Amidst photographs of the mangled steel and concrete of shopping malls, mosques, and residential buildings, the reader is tasked with looking closely—archaeologically—at the possibility of each window, and what was lost. —**Varun Nayar**

Lin Zhipeng

In his latest monograph, *Skinny Wave* (Same Paper, 2023; 254 pages, $50), Lin Zhipeng's keen eye for symbolism and everyday idiosyncrasies constructs a strange and vibrant world. Zhipeng, who also goes by 223, a moniker borrowed from the pining police officer in Wong Kar-wai's *Chungking Express*, is known for his dynamic photographs of Chinese youth culture—offbeat, colorful, and, more often than not, nude portraits of his friends that sit stylistically somewhere between the radical constructions of Ren Hang and the off-the-cuff, fashionable sensibility of Hiromix.

The magic of 223 lies in his ability to unite disparate subject matter through an attention to unusual and sublime patterns

Spread from Lin Zhipeng,
Skinny Wave (Same Paper,
2023)

of light, form, and color. In *Skinny Wave*, anonymous, nude figures appear and disappear within fecund forests, beaches, and rivers. It's a strange, vaguely Dionysian idea of nature: twisting branches, abundant flowers, an evocative splash of water against rock, each occasionally interrupted by signs of a world more recognizably modern—a flowering tree obscures the hood of a car, a dildo and hair dryer sit in an open desk drawer. Sometimes these two worlds merge. In one uncanny image, the smoke from a car engine blends into a cloud in the background. In this way, 223's photographs possess a hallucinatory quality similar to Wong's film.

The design of *Skinny Wave* complements 223's striking images. Four unique, overlapping, one-side-coated jackets enclose an open spine-bound book block. This layering continues in the interior, where sheets of uncoated paper fold out to reveal horizontal images, interspersed among the standard folios. With no text apart from the colophon, *Skinny Wave* is a testament to 223's ability to create an engaging, sensuous book carried by the power of image making. —**Noa Lin**

David Wojnarowicz

In the fall of 1978, a twenty-three-year-old David Wojnarowicz packed two bags and moved to Paris. It isn't surprising that an artist known, in part, for his photographs of figures wearing Arthur Rimbaud masks around New York was drawn to the French capital. He planned to live an artist's life there, to write a novel, to learn the language. He didn't write the novel, but he did fall deeply in love with a man named Jean Pierre Delage, whom he met at a cruising spot in the center of the city, near the Tuileries Garden. A six-month romance ensued. When Wojnarowicz returned to New York, he and Delage kept up an intense exchange of letters, filled with images, desires, and the humdrum details of their everyday lives.

Wojnarowicz's side of their three-year correspondence has now been collected in a dense, six-hundred-page tome that reads as an illustrated diary. The book, simply titled *Dear Jean Pierre* (**Primary Information, 2023; 616 pages, $40**), is an engrossing visual and epistolary chronology

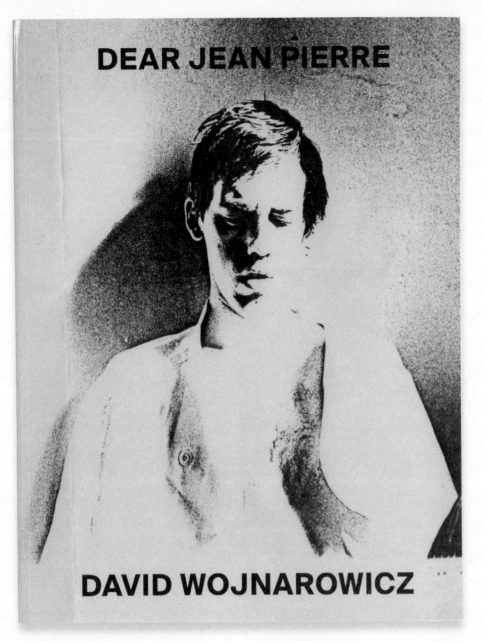

that reveals the artist's potent voice, the fits, starts, and frustrations of his early career, and his eye for imagery—through both his own work and postcard reproductions by everyone from Georgia O'Keeffe to Duane Michals. The book is a record of longing, loneliness, creative insecurity, and living precariously. Wojnarowicz always seems to be looking for a job or an apartment, or observing the extremes of the city's weather—it's hot, not so hot, it's cold. Perennial New York concerns. Some letters are abbreviated; others are bricks of typewritten text with no paragraph breaks. We read of parties, of wild living, the Pope's visit, New Wave bands on the ascent, wanderings on the waterfront, an encounter with Larry Clark's *Tulsa*, photographs that remind him of Jean Genet, a favorite outlaw writer. Across the book's many pages, we are reminded that Wojnarowicz was an artist who registered seemingly every vibration life offered, an artist the world lost far too soon.
—**Michael Famighetti**

Top and page 125: Cover and spread from David Wojnarowicz, *Dear Jean Pierre* (Primary Information, 2023); bottom: Cover of Aaron Turner, *Moves from the Archive* (Sleeper Studio, 2023)

Aaron Turner

Aaron Turner's ***Moves from the Archive*** (**Sleeper Studio, 2023; 86 pages, $50**) is the second offering in the Arkansas-based photographer's ongoing project *Black Alchemy Volumes 1, 2, and 3*. It's a compelling meditation on abstraction, the archive, and the possibilities of photographic art making—and in particular, Black art making.

As an object, the book is simultaneously unassuming and ambitious, taking the form of a thin paperback volume with an exposed spine and double-fold, die-cut cover—a reenactment in ink and paper of the fractured, trompe l'oeil gestures that animate the work within. The fifty-three duotone interior images are studio constructs, echoing László Moholy-Nagy's *Light-Space Modulator* images and drawing on a classically modernist ethos of experimentation and abstraction, albeit one fed via a distinct set of personal and cultural reference points. The studio set-ups feature projected, pinned, folded, and layered images drawn from family photographs and portraits of James Baldwin, Bayard Rustin, David Hammons, and Frederick Douglass, among other icons of Black art and politics. Each image is accompanied by a title that runs vertically along the gutter, dropping further references to artists such as Carrie Mae Weems, Sol LeWitt, and Georgia O'Keeffe. The various call-outs, both visual and textual, function as an invocation—a recipe of sorts. Add two parts Douglass to equal portions of Hammons, LeWitt, and Weems, and an alchemical reaction sets to boil.

In *There May Still Be Time Left* (2022), Turner's first volume within the *Black Alchemy* series, he asserts, "The photographs build a physical representation of my internal monologue . . . a continuation of moves that are native to me, foreign in meaning to the viewer, but recognizable in the method." In this second volume, the attentive viewer is ushered into a meticulously constructed image space and steeped in the artist's visual ponderings on art history, American history, and the image. It's a refreshing, entrancing book that leaves the viewer eager for the final volume. —**Lesley A. Martin**

RaMell Ross

In 2018, when the artist and filmmaker RaMell Ross sent out a Vimeo link to his film *Hale County This Morning, This Evening*, he implored viewers to use their best headphones, not a reedy laptop speaker. Every sound of his intimate documentary about Black life in Hale County, Alabama—which was nominated for an Oscar and has become one of the signal achievements of recent American cinema—was meant to be listened to with precision. Every thump of the basketball. Every revolution of the jump rope. Every outburst of thunder. Every spoken word or word misheard.

Ross's photographs likewise possess a surround-sound quality, one that relies on imagination or recollection of the American South. "To be an index, a document, a testament, a moment, a facsimile, a reference, a distillation, a memory," he writes in his monograph ***Spell, Time, Practice, American, Body*** (MACK, 2023; **252 pages, £50**), "of that physical and nonphysical region. To feel of the South, and Southern, like an accent can. To ring the Southern bell. Gonggg."

"Spell," the first of the book's five sections, opens with Ross's interrogative image of a hand holding an iPhone, a run-down, white-columned plantation house set in the camera's crosshairs. Ross's mysterious, often gestural portraits and scenes—a church steeple lying supine in a parking lot, a smiling child in the trunk of a car—appear in a steady sequence interrupted only by his poem "Slangless," a sly critique of Walker Evans and William Christenberry, who also chronicled Hale County and have long been totemic figures in Ross's imagination: "part ghost, part momentum."

From there, *Spell, Time* opens into four case studies that prove the expansive possibilities of the photobook as a vessel for forensics, video, sculpture, performance, and poetry. Ross breaks into a safe and discovers a cache of bullets and Confederate propaganda. He writes about the death of his mother and his discovery of photography. Designed like a schoolbook, with its riveted, three-hole-punch binding, *Spell, Time* is an assignment destined to be a classic, a claim on the future. —**Brendan Embser**

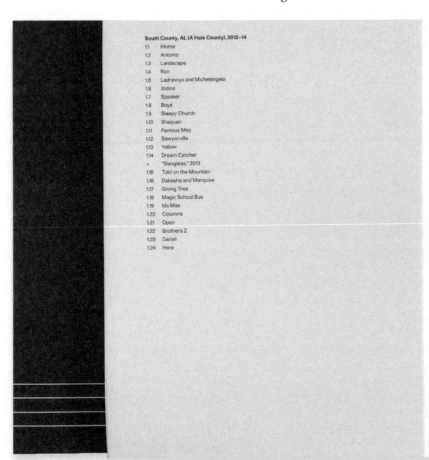

South County, AL (A Hale County), 2012–14

1.1 iHome
1.2 Antonio
1.3 Landscape
1.4 Ron
1.5 Ladrewya and Michelangelo
1.6 Jodice
1.7 Speaker
1.8 Boys
1.9 Sleepy Church
1.10 Shaquan
1.11 Famous Men
1.12 Sawyerville
1.13 Yellow
1.14 Dream Catcher
> "Slangless," 2013
1.15 Told on the Mountain
1.16 Dakesha and Marquise
1.17 Giving Tree
1.18 Magic School Bus
1.19 Ida Mae
1.20 Columns
1.21 Open
1.22 Brothers Z
1.23 Daniel
1.24 Here

Endnote
Patrick Radden Keefe

As an investigative journalist and author of engrossing nonfiction, Patrick Radden Keefe has mined irresistible stories of rogues, kingpins, and the Sackler family's sordid complicity with the opioid-addiction crisis. His 2018 book, *Say Nothing*, revisits the history of the Troubles, in Northern Ireland. Fittingly, given its memorable characters and surreal events, the book will soon be adapted as a television series.

Chris Steele-Perkins, Outside Divis Flats, West Belfast, Northern Ireland, 1978
© the artist/Magnum Photos

Say Nothing: A True Story of Murder and Memory in Northern Ireland **features numerous photographs, including one of Dolours Price, the Provisional Irish Republican Army (IRA) volunteer who was photographed in the 1970s for the Italian publication *L'Europeo*. How did her image make it onto the cover of your book?**
I've been working for the last several years on a limited dramatic series based on the book, which I'm producing. So, this question of image and self-presentation has been very much on my mind. Dolours Price was attuned to the iconography of revolutionary glamour. That was helpful for me in understanding her as a character but also the way seductive imagery could pull people into radical politics. She and many of her contemporaries were obsessed with Che Guevara, and specifically with photos of Che.

What role did photography play in your writing?
I've always used photography in my research. If I'm trying to find a way to inhabit a time period I did not experience firsthand, photographs are just one especially vivid piece of the archival puzzle.

The Magnum photographer Chris Steele-Perkins worked in Northern Ireland in the late 1970s. What did you see as evocative about his photographs of the Belfast housing complex—and IRA stronghold—Divis Flats?
Chris Steele-Perkins captures the sense of antic life that continued even against the backdrop of terrible violence and carnage. One of the most extraordinary things about photos from the '70s in Belfast is that you'll have an armored personnel carrier, or a soldier with a rifle, or a checkpoint, and then, in the corners of the frame, you just see all these kids, kind of hanging out, playing. To me, that speaks of the irrepressibility of the place, and the way in which, even in the direst of times, life goes on.

As a journalist, do you typically view photographs as evidence or with a sense of skepticism?
I think of them as artifacts. I'm trying in my work to close the distance between the reader and the people I'm writing about, to create a kind of intimacy with my subjects, and photography is incredibly helpful in that respect.

Arrigo Benedetti, the cofounder of *L'Europeo*, said that "people look at articles, but read the photos." Tragically, it seems there's only one known photograph of Jean McConville, a young widow who was disappeared from Divis Flats in 1972—and whose fate was intertwined with Dolours Price's.
Jean was a mother of ten and a widow and poor. Only the one photo survives. And her children all have copies of it. Jean has this iconic status as a victim of the Troubles, but she's not a full-fleshed character in the way that some of the others in my book are. What she does is she disappears. In the process of making the television series of *Say Nothing*, you end up kind of coloring in between the lines. We cast an actress as Jean McConville. We give her dialogue. And there may be a kind of hubris in that, but I think there's a thoughtful and responsible way to do it.

Do you feel that photographs—personal, archival, documentary—can tell an alternate history?
One of the big subjects that I keep coming back to as a writer is denial. Whether it's personal denial, or denial in the context of family, or denial writ large on a national, societal level. And in many of these instances, the things I'm trying to take a hard look at are things that other people are hoping to avert their eyes from. To me, one thread that connects those different types of images and the counterhistories they suggest is that there's a sense of defiance. A sense that it's impossible to look away.